MW00897667

Death Shadow: Chri.

An Analytical Investigation Leading to a Proposal for a Christian
Purification Rite to Minister to Veterans Suffering from
Posttraumatic Stress Injury.

David L. Bachelor

A thesis for the degree of

Doctor of Philosophy

At

Trinity Theological Seminary

Newburgh, IN

USA

ABSTRACT

I am studying the way the Christian church ministers to veterans returning from war. I want to discover if there is a missing element in the current approach to veterans' ministries in order to alleviate the problems many veterans experience in reconnecting to God, the church, and the community. It is my hope that we in the Church will not allow the creation of another generation of lost veterans similar to the one that emerged after the Vietnam War.

DISCLAIMER

The views expressed in this paper that are not attributed to another source are either my own or endorsed by me. Nothing in this work should be considered official policy of the United Methodist Church or any branch of the Department of Defense unless it is a quotation from an official publication of these organizations.

This study is not endorsed by any branch of the U.S Government. This includes the Department of Defense and specifically the U.S. Navy.

All rights reserved.

ISBN-10: 1499280653
ISBN-13: 978-1499280654

DEDICATION

To the Veterans of the Vietnam War:

When I was a young man, you trained me for war. Thirty years later, you met me at the airport as I returned from Operation Iraqi Freedom. You made sure today's veterans have a hero's homecoming because you never received one.

I would also like to dedicate this work to Jonathan Shay and David Bosworth. Without their pioneering works, this study would not have been possible. Thank you both for your labor.

Bible Translations used in this work:

This publication contains The Holy Bible, English Standard Version®, copyright ©2001 by Crossway Bibles, a publishing ministry of Good News Publishers. ESV Text Edition: 2007. The ESV® text has been reproduced in cooperation with and by permission of Good News Publishers. Unauthorized reproduction of this publication is prohibited.

Scriptures marked as "(BBE)" are taken from The Bible in Basic English. This translation is in the public domain.

Scriptures marked as "(CEV)" are taken from the Contemporary English Version © 1995 by American Bible Society. Used by permission.

Scriptures marked as "(GNB)" are taken from the Good News Bible – Second Edition © 1992 by American Bible Society. Used by permission.

Scriptures marked as "(MKJV)" are taken from the Holy Bible, Modern King James Version
Copyright © 1962 - 1998
By Jay P. Green, Sr.
Used by permission of the copyright holder.

In this book any Scripture that is not identified by translation is taken from the MKJV.

Cover created by:

PortraitEFX – North San Antonio
1739 SW Loop 410 Suite #804-163, San Antonio, TX, 78227, USAPhone: 210-323-1794

http://nsanantonio.portraitefx.com/

CONTENTS

INTRODUCTION

He restoreth my soul; He guideth me in straight paths for His name's sake. Yea, though I walk through the valley of the shadow of death, I will fear no evil, for Thou art with me; Thy rod and Thy staff, they comfort me. Thou preparest a table before me in the presence of mine enemies; Thou hast anointed my head with oil; my cup runneth over. (Ps 23:3-5 JPS)

So they're medical boarding me here in the next few months and they're really not giving me much to say in it. So, instead of taking a bad turn and a bad attitude, I'm going to keep a positive attitude on this; keep going to counseling, keep taking my medicine, and keep sowing into these three lives right here, and reach out and help every veteran I can.[1]

> Religious Programs Specialist Chief (RPC) Bob Page
> USNR, veteran of Operation Iraqi
> Freedom/Operation Enduring Freedom

Over three millennia have passed since King David celebrated God's power to restore his soul after a tour in the shadow of death. More than just keeping him safe, God made David's enemies watch while David enjoyed security and abundance. Iraqi War veteran Bob Page, the Navy Religious Programs Specialist Chief quoted above, has no such expectation. Even though his military specialty involved daily contact with senior level chaplains, he has resigned himself to managing his war-experiences through a regimen of counseling, good works and pharmaceutical relief. RPC Page's coping strategy is a reflection of current practices in the chaplain corps of all branches of the military for warriors with Posttraumatic Stress Injury.[2]

The clinical (and thus official) name for symptoms of traumatic stress that persist longer than 30 days after the traumatic event is Post Traumatic Stress Disorder. This study objects to the word "disorder" as an appropriate term for what is a wound. Due to this objection, and as an attempt to change the clinical label for this injury, there will be no use of the term "Post Traumatic Stress Disorder" or the initials

"PTSD" within the body of this study. When clinical trials or official documents are referenced, the editing of PTSD to PTSI will have already occurred. When cited in footnotes or in the bibliography the original spelling and/or terminology has been used.

The earlier observation that RPC Page's coping strategy reflects the current practices of military ministry is not meant to condemn chaplains. Every U.S. military chaplain is endorsed by a civilian faith group whose beliefs and practices the chaplain is pledged to reflect in his or her military ministry.[3] Thus, if a belief or practice is missing in military chaplaincy it is because it is missing in the American Christian community. Somewhere between the campaigns of King David and the battlefields of Iraq and Afghanistan, American Christians lost the expectation that God could walk veterans through the psychological aspect of the shadow of death.

Not all churches even want to minister to veterans as "veterans". Those that are willing to engage in this outreach usually provide some combination of special services, prayers and appropriate-for-the-context scripture verses. If this formula fails to bring relief, then military chaplains and the modern church consider themselves to have exhausted their spiritual arsenal and refer the veteran to the medical community. The example of RPC Page is just one of thousands. This study intends to show that modern warriors need to have their inner-self restored after their war-experiences as much as the ancient king of Israel, and that if they receive it, these veterans will no longer bear the shadow of death upon their lives.

In order to understand how ministry to veterans has been conducted by God's people, this study will examine every model present in Scripture. The purpose and method of each interaction will be codified. This list will be compared with the current ministries offered by the Christian community to see if there is any discrepancy that might explain the inability to restore warriors. This study will demonstrate that exposure to extreme events like war can alter the fabric of a warrior's material and immaterial makeup. The evidence for this has been gathered from medical, military and theological sources. Keeping the focus on the plasticity of the human self, this study will show that the missing element in ministry to war veterans is a purification process.

Using Numbers 19:14 as the core verse, in which anything within a place of death is expressed as being polluted, it will be shown that "death-shadow" is a pre-modern assessment of the condition now known as Posttraumatic Stress Injury. Other texts from the Hebrew Scriptures will demonstrate that the ancient Hebrews recognized the pathological properties of this affliction. Scriptural evidence from the New Testament will show that Jesus' priesthood contains a specific charter for the cleansing from death-shadow. Tapping into Jesus' charter for purifying war-tainted veterans, this study will conclude by offering a model for purification from death-shadow that will complete the pattern established in Scripture for the restoration of the deepest parts of a warrior.

Importance of the Study

> The essential feature of Posttraumatic Stress [Injury] is the development of characteristic symptoms following exposure to an extreme traumatic stressor involving direct personal experience of an event that involves actual or threatened death or serious injury, or other threat to one's physical integrity. ..[4]

In 2008, the Rand Corporation conducted a study on the incidence of Posttraumatic Stress Injury (PTSI) among the 1.64 million veterans of Operation Enduring Freedom (Afghanistan) and Operation Iraqi Freedom (Iraq).[5] The researchers estimate that at least 300,000 of these veterans will develop PTSI or major depression.[6] The data used in the Rand study is now more than four years old. At least three hundred thousand additional warriors have deployed in the intervening years. With a projected incidence rate for mental disorders among these returning veterans of 26 percent,[7] these past four years have potentially generated tens of thousands of additional cases of major depression and PTSI walking the streets of America.

In order to be diagnosed with PTSI, the *Diagnostic and Statistical*

Manual of Mental Disorders (*DSM-IV-TR*) requires that a person have been exposed to deadly environment.[8] Death and the possibility of death is an emotional stressor.[9] The possibility of death exists anywhere in a war zone. As the *Iraq War Clinician Guide* states , "The destructive force of war creates an atmosphere of chaos and compels service members to face the terror of unexpected injury, loss, and death."[10] Thus all deployed personnel have the potential to develop PTSI.

The stress caused by being exposed to death is not a recent development but has been noted in the writings of the ancient world.[11] This study will suggest that the Hebrew Scriptures contain accounts of people who developed PTSI as a result of death-exposure and that the Hebrews knew this injury as "death-shadow." This study will also suggest that Scripture contains a remedy for death-exposure. The war narratives in Hebrew Scripture reflect an inclusive attitude towards death-exposure and require both combatants and non-combatants to be treated for its effects.[12] Without "treatment" veterans were cut-off from God's presence.

Separation from God is still a common side-effect of PTSI. Psychological studies have shown that, "One of the most pervasive effects of traumatic exposure is the challenge that people experience to their existential beliefs concerning the meaning and purpose of life, particularly at risk is the strength of their religious faith and the comfort that they derive from it."[13] The timeless quality of this ,reaction to combat is illustrated in the Psalms when a war veteran says to God, "But you have rejected us and disgraced us and have not gone out with our armies"(Ps 44:9). Some secular experts on PTSI attribute the spiritual separation of war to the veteran's perception of contamination. Clinical psychologist Ed Tick notes, "The pollution we accumulate through participation in war interrupts our connection to the Divine."[14] Dr. Tick's observation is echoed by Biblical scholar David Bosworth. In his study of King David, Dr. Bosworth concludes that present day "[v]eterans feel contaminated with no way of becoming pure."[15] Dr. Bosworth suggests that "religious communities" institute purification rituals as part of the therapy provided to veterans.[16] Department of Veterans Affairs psychiatrist Jonathan Shay echoes this call for a purification ritual with "religious force" in order to restore veterans who have been injured by their exposure to a deadly environment.[17]

Although Tick, Bosworth and Shay believe in the power of purification rituals, the problem for Christian veterans with "death-exposure" contamination is that the Church has no way to make them "clean." As Dr. Bosworth notes, "[S]ince American veterans live in a society that has no explicit system of purity, they have no access to purification."[18] This is in contrast to some non-Christian cultures that have purification rituals. The most familiar in America are Native American sweat lodges. Even Judaism used to offer cleansing from death-shadow in ancient times. The nineteenth chapter of the book of Numbers contains the parameters for death contamination and how to be purified from the contagion. Unfortunately the destruction of the Second Temple rendered that process inaccessible.[19] But even if that technique were still in use, Christianity operates according to the view expressed in *The Holman Illustrated Bible Dictionary* that "[Jesus'] atoning death . . . transcended all the Law's cleansing rituals . . . in the single offering of Himself for us on Calvary."[20] To re-institute any of the purification rituals found in the Torah would appear to be a step away from the freedom from the law purchased at the Cross.[21] Yet the problem of veterans seeking purification is real. As Dr. Shay notes, ". . . in modern American life few veterans have found purification, although many have sought it in suicide."[22]

Suicide is still a very real threat to warriors. In the first half of 2012 all branches of the military were on track to have more suicides in 2012 than any previous year.[23] Among Vietnam War veterans there is an ongoing debate about the suicide rate of these warriors.[24] What is an established fact is that PTSI and suicide are linked together in the mind of some veterans of Vietnam and current wars.[25] For those veterans who think that suicide is the only way to be purified of their PTSI, this study will offer another way.

Even though the *DSM-IV TR* names exposure to a deadly environment as the trigger for PTSI, some supporters of a veterans' purification ritual think that blood-guilt is the agent that must be purged. Dr. Jonathan Shay and Dr. David Bosworth, working separately and in completely different disciplines, have both looked at the subject of war-pollution and arrived at a similar conclusion. Dr. Shay sees a need for American society to establish a ritual for veterans because, ". . . *everyone* who has shed blood, no matter how blamelessly, is in need of purification."[26] Dr. Bosworth also believes "killing in war can interfere with the soldier's relationship with God" and suggests a biblically-based purification ceremony to alleviate some of a veteran's blood-guilt.[27] Many military-specific ministries also focus on the infliction of harm as the cause for PTSI. In the instructional manual for pastors and churches provided by the Elim Lutheran Church of Blackhoof, Minnesota, Christians are taught that, "One does not have to be a direct participant in violent acts to experience the wounding of soul and conscience."[28] Both secular and Christian authorities attribute veterans' contamination to their association with slaughter.

Instead of "killing" or "blood-guilt", this study will propose "death-exposure" as the contaminant that keeps veterans from full reconnection to God and society after their time in war. In the only New Testament reference to Numbers 19, Hebrew believers are promised that the blood of Jesus cleanses a person's "conscience" from "works of death."(Heb 9:14) This study proposes a way to inaugurate death-exposure purification to the family of Christian ministries. When death-exposure is not cleansed, and the veteran continues to re-experience their brush with death, this study proposes that the Hebrew Scripture called this injury "death-shadow" (צלמות). In order to restore people wounded by death-exposure to a relationship with God and their neighbor, this study will propose a rite based on the veterans' quarantine in Numbers 31, and concluding with the pre-combat purification Jesus performed for his disciples in John 13. Jesus told his followers that they did not understand what he was doing that night, but they would later (Jn 13:7). This study proposes that this time has come.

Organization of the Study

War is not a new phenomenon, but the diagnosis of Post-traumatic Stress Injury is limited to the last thirty years. This study will take an in-depth look at the material and immaterial manifestations of war-related PTSI in a human being. Since PTSI is a recently created term, this study will suggest that God revealed a Hebrew word (צלמות

'death-shadow'[29]) for this injury during the era of Abraham. To illustrate the similarities between this term and traumatic stress injury, Psalm 44 and Mark 5 will be critiqued according to the filters established by therapists with experience working with PTSI. These two narratives were chosen for their relation to the word צלמות , the presence of veterans, and the expectation that God could heal this injury.

Using the clinical standards set for this malady in *DSM-IV-TR,* the entire Scriptures will be scrutinized to identify which persons in Biblical narratives have characteristics similar to deployment-related PTSI. The various processes and rites used by the Levites and laity of ancient Israel to minister to veterans will be catalogued. After each type of ministry is described and its location in Scripture cited, some current examples of similar veterans' ministries in American Christianity will be listed. It will be evident from this exercise that several ancient ministries are absent from veterans' ministries in the U.S. Most notable is death-exposure purification ministry.

To validate the efficacy of veterans' purification rites in the process of veteran reintegration to society, this study will showcase two modern non-Christian rites that employ cleansing ceremonies as part of the process of warrior re-integration in civic life. After the inspection of these processes, this study will propose a rite for the Church to re-introduce death-exposure purification ministry for veterans. An order of service will be presented to facilitate the conversion from an ancient Levitical ceremony to a modern Christian ministry. The proposal will include the narrative to be used by the person presiding at the ceremony, as well as a list of suggested mementos to aid the veterans in their inner-cleansing. There will be guidelines for the selection of officiates and participants.

The final portion of the study will be the conclusion and suggestions for the Church to restore death-exposure purification to veterans' ministry.

DELIMITATIONS

Biblical Names: For clarity's sake, the final version of a person's name in Scripture will be the form used for all references in the body of this study without regard to the form of their name at the time of a particular narrative. Ex: "Abraham" will be used in place of "Abram" even though this shorter version is the form of his name in the narrative of Genesis 14. Unless otherwise noted, all Scripture quoted is from the Modern King James Version (MKJV) translation.

Veteran Purification: It is an a priori assumption of this study that war veterans have been exposed to death, regardless of whether an individual has seen combat or not. The corollary to this assumption is that God intends for the Church to have a role in the purification of veterans from death-exposure. This is because the forerunner to the Church, the tabernacle, had a role in cleansing the veterans of ancient Israelite military campaigns. Jesus also ministered to veterans.

Death-Exposure: In the First Covenant corpse-uncleanness, or "death-exposure" as it is called in this study, was a form of "ritual" or "cultic" uncleanness. "The list of impurity bearers in the Torah [is] - the "leper," gonorrheic, corpse-contaminated, childbearer, emitter of semen, and menstruant (Nu 5:14; Lev 12; 15:16-24)."[30] These biological conditions where labeled as "error" or חטאה, and prevented a person from participation in cultic functions of the temple or tabernacle. These organic states rendered a person "unclean" (טמא) but were not a moral infraction against God. This study will not address itself to whether "ritual" purity, and practices like "churching" women, that are still practiced in some parts of the Church, really belong in the practice of Christian faith under the Final Covenant. Rather this study will concern itself only with one type of biological impurity from the First Covenant, death-exposure, and address this issue as an injury to the inner-self under the Final Covenant.

Death as an obstacle to God: This study will not attempt to explain why "death" is complementary but separate from "sin" as an impediment to God's presence. The alteration of the biological fabric of a person by exposure to death is documented in a later chapter of this study. Also documented is the alteration of a person's relationship with God because of exposure to death.

The Epistle to the Hebrews: A central pillar of this study is the teachings contained in the Epistle to the Hebrews. There has been debate within Christianity whether this epistle is an authentic portion of the Christian canon. This study will not address any of the issues associated with these contentions: authorship, canonicity, authority, intended audience, etc. This study accepts this epistle as "God-breathed" and draws conclusions accordingly.

Efficacy of ordinances or sacraments: There is disagreement in the Church concerning God's participation in baptism, the Lord's Table and other rites from the ministry of Jesus. The view of this study is that God's participation in any rite is larger than the human contribution, and more importantly, God is the one who accomplishes whatever purpose the rite reflects. This study will not address whether these acts require human sacerdotal participation to be effective or have divine consequence because of human obedience to God's word. It is the position of this study that no person or situation remains unchanged when God is invited, through rite or prayer, to participate.

Morality of war: This study will not examine the morality of war according to the understanding of man. It is undeniable in the Scriptures of both First and Final Covenants that war is one of the instrument God uses to accomplish his purpose. Having asserted this point, this study does not condone all wars, but does reject any teaching that holds all wars to be intrinsically evil.

"Warzone" vs "Combat" as a Stressor: Since it is impossible to predict how much death-exposure will overwhelm a person's faculties and leave them a casualty of war, this study will not draw a distinction between combat-stress and warzone-stress. It is the position of this study that deployment to a warzone implies exposure to death, without any necessity to engage in combat, therefore only "warzone-stress" will be used to name the secular precursor to PTSI.

<u>KEY TERMS</u>:

Christendom-
The various peoples and groups who identify themselves and their practices as "Christian".

Christian-
A person or people who self-identify as "Christian" when asked to identify their religion. No other measurement of fidelity is applied or assumed. When used in conjunction with the term "Christendom", "Christian" is then a cultural term.

Church-
The collective label for all Christians who practice their faith now (or at any time) in any group, association, or community.

Church Age
The time period that began with the death of the last person who had experienced Jesus' terrestrial life and ministry.

Cognitions
Concepts understood and transmitted by an individual in the sentient portions of their body.

Contaminate:
1) To soil, stain, corrupt or infect by contact or association. 2) To make unfit for use by the introduction of unwholesome or undesirable elements.[31]

Death-Exposure:
Contact at any level to dead people, and/or the possibility of death, and/or an environment where death is the primary purpose of large numbers of participants.

Death-shadow-
Derived from צלמות in Psalm 44:19, it is the injury caused by death-exposure. In this study the proposed Biblical name for PTSI.

Depression:

"The gross changes in cognitive organization that lead to incorrect information processing [and] result . . .[in] a wide variety of painful symptoms."[32]

First Covenant:
Sometimes referred to in Christendom as the Old Testament. In this study "First Covenant" and "Hebrew Scriptures" refer to the 39 books accepted as canonical by all major branches of Judaism and Christianity.

Final Covenant:
The twenty seven books still commonly called the New Testament. In this study the terms "Christian Scriptures" and "Final Covenant" refer to the books that are not part of the Hebrew canon but are recognized as canonical by all major branches of the Christian Church.

Grief:
Stress caused by the loss of someone who is cared about, such as a buddy, leader, or family member.

Moral Injury:
The lasting psychological, biological, spiritual, behavioral, and social impact of perpetrating, failing to prevent, or bearing witness to acts that transgress deeply held moral beliefs and expectations.[33]

Posttraumatic Stress Injury (PTSI):
A traumatic stress injury that fails to heal such that the symptoms and behaviors it causes remain significantly troubling or disabling beyond 30 days after their onset.

Nephesh
Pertaining to the immaterial component of a person. This includes sentient processes like thinking and memory; appetites and desires; character and identity.

Stress Adaptation:
The normal, reversible coping process using positive action or allowing the nephesh to atrophy. Stress adaptation is always temporary, and disappears when the environment no longer requires the adaptation.

Stressor:
Any challenge or set of challenges to the material or immaterial components of a person.

Traumatic Stress Injury:
The potentially irreversible changes to the nephesh and body of a human being, due to death-exposure, that exceed in intensity or duration the ability of the individual to adapt.

Veteran:
A former member of the military, a former warrior and/or a person who has experienced armed conflict.

Warrior:
A member of a group whose purpose is to engage in hostile acts against an opponent. This includes all members of the armed services of any government. It also includes tribal, clan and family-based irregular forces.

Warzone Stress:
Changes in body and nephesh functioning and/or behavior due to the challenges encountered in a warzone.

CHAPTER 1

Statement of the Problem

The people that walked in darkness have seen a great light:
they that dwell in the land of the shadow of death (צלמות)
upon them hath the light shined. (Isa 9:2)

And you, child, will be named the prophet of the Most High:
you will go before the face of the Lord, to make ready his
ways; To give knowledge of salvation to his people, through
the forgiveness of sins . . .To give light to those in dark
places, and in the shadow of death, so that our feet may be
guided into the way of peace. (Lk 1:76-79 BBE)

According to the *Diagnostic and Statistical Manual of Mental Disorders,
4th Edition, Text Revised* (*DSM-IV-TR*), which is the clinical standard set
by the American Psychiatric Association, being over-shadowed by
death is the first criterion for Posttraumatic Stress Injury (PTSI).[34]
PTSI is the most common wound found in modern veterans of
Operation Enduring Freedom and Operation Iraqi Freedom.[35] The
prophet Isaiah is the only writer in the Hebrew canon God inspired to
see the cure for the wound caused by exposure to death. Centuries later
God shared that inspiration with the father of John the Baptist as the
above quotes demonstrate. Zechariah saw that Jesus would bring: (1)
remission for violations of God's ordinances; and (2) illumination to
people over-shadowed by exposure to death. After the conclusion of
Jesus' earthly ministry, an anonymous writer re-stated for the Church
Age how Jesus fulfilled these twin vocations.

In the ninth chapter of the unsigned Letter to the Hebrews,
believers are told that the blood of Jesus purges the conscience of
"works of death."[36] The previous verse (9:13) sets the context of this
decontamination within a culture that included priests and cultic

washings as a regular feature of life. [37] In precedence over "the blood of bulls and of goats" which was for moral infractions (Nu 15:22-24) and "the ashes of a heifer sprinkling the unclean" which was the cleanser for death-exposure (Nu 19:17; Nu 31:19), the author of Hebrews informs his Judaica-inclined readers that the blood of Jesus is the new and better sanitizer for a conscience containing contamination because of sin or exposure to deadly conditions. Now in the twenty-first century of its existence, the Church no longer accesses the blood of Jesus for the shadow deadly situations can inflict on a person's conscience. It has focused all purification ministries to address sin-pollution, including those for returning veterans with PTSI.

The Early Church

The trend towards a sin-oriented process for veterans began very early in the history of the Church. Bernard J. Verkamp writes in *The Moral Treatment of Returning Warriors in Early Medieval and Modern Times* that, "[T]here evolved out of the notion of cultic purity a sense of inward purity of the heart . ... Impurity, in other words, was transferred inward and came to be associated with sin."[38] The rejection of warfare, as violating the 5th commandment and possibly the New Testament restriction against "blood"[39], is considered by most scholars to have been standard practice.[40] Some of the early church leaders, such as Tertullian and Origen, considered blood-guilt to be an "irremissable" sin, and thus beyond the reach of human agency.[41] Tertullian was not just concerned with those who engaged in combat. Citing the conflict between vows to the state and the inner loyalty required of a Christian to Jesus alone, Tertullian viewed every aspect of military service, including guard duty, as sin.[42]

The climate of pacifism in the early Church was undone by the battle of the Milvian Bridge in 312 C.E.[43] Legend has it that the Roman Emperor Constantine received a vision that showed him a cross and told him, "by this sign conquer."[44] Constantine's embrace of Christianity altered the structure of military service in the Roman Empire. Soldiers no longer were required to participate in pagan rituals that deified the emperor instead of Christ. The termination of this practice removed a major impediment for Christians to serve in the Roman Legions.[45] In fact, by 416 C.E. only Christians could serve in the Roman military.[46] Although the increase in enlistments changed the public's perception of Christians in the military, it was the writings of Augustine of Hippo that changed the Church's theology about war.[47]

According to Augustine, the "wise man" (meaning "Christian") had a duty to wage war to resist injustice.[48] Done as a duty, it was morally neutral, and did not need purification.[49] But this duty did not give Christians license to fight in a manner that was immoral or evil.[50] It was not the outward act for Augustine that constituted the uncleanness, but a person's inner attitude.[51] Augustine, building on the earlier works of many philosophers and theologians, enumerated the conditions that legitimized military action by the state: 1) War must have a just cause; 2) War must be declared by rightful authority; War must be waged with right intention.[52] Those conditions are referred to, in modern parlance, as the Just War Theory.[53] The Latin word used by Augustine for his first condition is "jus." This Latin word means "just" in the sense of "right" and "legal." By establishing a juridical standard for the conduct of war, Augustine eliminated the death pollution of chapters 19 and 31 in Numbers as a possible outcome from war. Augustine's use of a legal paradigm also set in motion the idea of restitution by the guilty party. As one modern scholar comments "Plain justice demands that we right the wrongs that we do to the best of our ability."[54] In the early and medieval Church this was manifested in the practice of purification known as penance.[55]

With the development of "penance", Bernard Verkamp believes the Christian Church had found a substitute for cleansing veterans with "the ashes of a heifer".[56] Darrell Clay, in his article, "Just War, Penance and the Church" agrees with Verkamp's connection between Numbers 31 and penance. Both authors try to connect penance with *horror sanguiness*, the primeval superstition associated with shedding blood, but Verkamp and Clay eventually concede that penance had less to do with cultic purity than atoning for guilt.[57] Clay endorses the tradition and practice of penance for military veterans, "Should the church fail to discipline one who has violated the moral order, further violations may result. This is especially true in warfare, which is brutal enough as it is and very susceptible to progressive immorality. The church has to be the church, so its members cannot live viciously."[58] This insight into Clay's thinking confirms that penance does not address the death-exposure aspect of Numbers 31. Nothing in the Hebrew text suggests that the female virgin prisoners-of-war were "vicious." Yet these girls had to undergo the same purification as the warriors who had slain the girls' fathers and brothers (Nu 31:19).

In the earliest attempt to levy penance on veterans, the common sanction was withholding the elements of the communion table. In the fourth century Basil the Great recommended that warriors who had shed blood, "abstain from communion for three years."[59] In the centuries that followed a genre of instructive manuals for penance developed called "penitentials."[60] Initially these writings equated slaying enemy soldiers on the battlefield with homicide, but by the late seventh century a distinction was made for soldiers who killed at the command of their leader or "in a public war."[61] The standard purification process for these guilty warriors was 40 days of fasting and humiliation.[62] Not only did penance absolve the guilt from the warrior, but through these exercises the veteran "recover[ed] the favor of God."[63]

No longer officially called the Sacrament of Penance, the Roman Catholic Church still offers a form of purification that would grant the same absolution from blood-guilt to veterans. The modern title of this ministry is the Sacrament of Reconciliation. The two components or "signs" of the sacrament confirm that it is still a "sin" oriented purification rite. The two "signs" are the participant's sorrow for their actions, in this case the warrior's deeds while on deployment, and the priest's words of absolution. "The church teaches that when we perform these outward signs, our sins are washed away, and we are made right with God once more."[64] Although Protestants initially shared some of the same ideas about penance[65], the consensus of most non-Catholics changed after the Enlightenment, and Protestants have largely discontinued the practice of ecclesiastical authorities imposing temporal sanctions in the context of absolution.[66]

The Protestant Church

Modern Protestants may lack the concept of "penance" but there are Protestant versions of sin-purification ministries to help veterans deal with "works of death." New ministries are springing up every day to help decontaminate the tide of returning warriors. Sometimes the "sin" is assigned to enemy soldiers, because the foe's guilt can have repercussions for American veterans. For example, Military Ministry counselor Chris Adsit tells the wife of a wounded warrior, "Your husband's condition is due to the sinful actions of men – not God."[67] Adsit does not call the veteran with PTSI a sinner, but does assign the root of this malady to rebellion against God. In his manual, which not only has the endorsement of Military Ministry but also large networks of Protestant churches, there are 'exercises" that are sin-purification rituals in all but name. The simplest is an exercise called "spiritual breathing." The first step to "exhale" is confessing personal sins. The *Manual* deepens the metaphorical use of respiration, a few paragraphs later with, the illustration of a drowning man expelling the water in his lungs. The contamination of past actions has progressed in this metaphor from a harmful gas to a substance that actually blocks the veteran from receiving what he or she needs to live.[68] Learning to "spiritually breathe" removes those impurities and is recommended, "As often as you need to . . . once a week, once a day, once an hour or even once every few minutes!"[69]

Another form of purging recommended by Military Ministry is journaling. Adsit suggests that veterans write down as much as they can remember of the incident at the root of their trauma. Instead of "respiration," Adsit uses different metaphors to describe the spiritual pollution addressed by this particular rite. Journaling helps veterans own the memories they have been hiding in their subconscious that are like a "computer virus" or "splinter in your finger."[70] By completing this exercise these foreign objects at the root of the veteran's PTSI will be ejected.[71] Quoting David Grossman, an expert on the effects of combat, Adsit assures his readers, "You're only as sick as your secrets."[72] If journaling is not sufficient, then the *Manual* offers a "Memorial Project." This rite also starts off with a written confession as the veteran makes a list of his or her sins and puts it in a jar. The list is burned and the jar is then sealed. It is a "memorial" to God's forgiveness of confessed sin which allows the veteran to declare, " I am clean before God."[73]

Elim Lutheran Church of Blackhoof, Minnesota has a pastoral ministry that uses the book *Welcome Them Home Help Them Heal.* The book is recommended by the Department of Defense. The recommended first step of the "Transition from Soldier to Citizen", which is the title of the book's second chapter, is "shedding" elements from the combat zone.[74] The authors are referring to the psychogenic aspects that prevent safe re-integration to civilian society. In the context of the chapter, which deals with the immediate reactions to post-deployment, it is clear that "shedding" is a euphemism setting the stage for later purification exercises.

According to *Welcome Them Home*, a wide spectrum of behaviors, thought processes, and experiences must be "shed" or purged from the returning warrior. In these early pages of the book the sin basis of the purification is not mentioned. Only as spiritual topics surface does "shedding" mean confessing. "In the Christian tradition, war has long been regarded as a gross consequence of human failure."[75] The first rite encourages the veteran to create a lamentation. This is defined as "a personal poem of pain and grief."[76] Although this does not require a confession, the bullet points provided offer guilt and shame as possible material for the lament and the rite concludes with the analogy that "our broken relationship with God and each other [is] symbolized graphically in the images of war."[77]

After the veteran has lamented, the next stage for this warrior is telling the "story", which may contain "pronounced guilt and shame."[78] *Welcome Them Home* warns church members who are part of the "story" process that "Veterans seeking forgiveness and reconciliation after war-related trauma bear heavy burdens.. . When a veteran delves into confessional material . . . listeners need to be prepared for disturbing accounts and intense emotional release" (p.70). This may lead the veteran to ask for a formal purification rite like Confession and Reconciliation.[79] The book advocates a series of rituals that churches should provide to veterans throughout the liturgical year and offers a proto-type called the "Advent Heart-Cleansing Ritual." This rite builds up to a confessional prayer and a symbolic purging gesture of burning slips of paper containing past emotional wounds.[80] Its purpose is "identifying and letting go of obstacles that separate us from God and from one another."[81] The recommendation is for churches to conduct this ceremony at the start of Advent in either November or December and repeat it at Lent.[82]

Some alternative forms of sin purification in Protestant veterans' ministry encourage ministers to be a surrogate and confess the sins of the warrior. Operation Barnabas has the leader of their liturgy confess, "Where our brothers and sisters in uniform have stumbled and done that which is not pleasing in your sight, grant your rich Word of forgiveness."[83] The Presbyterian Church, U.S.A. instructs their worship leaders to anticipate guilt "haunting many returning veterans" and to construct appropriate "public confession" to absolve the warriors of their culpability.[84] The United Methodist Church has the minister suggest to its veterans that they may have acted ". . . outside the parameters of civilized behavior."[85] The Methodist liturgy then allows a few moments of silence for the warriors to be more specific in their confession to God before the minister gives the assurance of pardon. These are just three examples of surrogate confession rites but countless other variations are in use throughout Christianity. Sometimes even the ministers are guilty for their ministry to warriors. In an article by the United Methodist News Service, the reporter began her story about a group of military chaplains with the words, "In the name of Jesus Christ you are forgiven."[86]

CHAPTER 2

Warzone PTSI

Though hostilities cease and though life moves on, and though loved ones yearn for their healing, veterans often remain drenched in the imagery and emotion of war for decades and sometimes for their entire lives.[87]

Contaminate: (1) To soil, stain, corrupt or infect by contact or association.(2) To make unfit for use by the introduction of unwholesome or undesirable elements.[88]

Therapists believe that Posttraumatic Stress Injury (PTSI) develops when a person's biology and his or her understanding of the world render him or her unable to process an event.[89] This means that PTSI has both a material and an immaterial component. Clinically speaking, a person with PTSI has been "hurt" after his or her exposure to an environment where "wounds" are a possibility. This definition is merely a deconstruction of the component parts of the term "PTSI." "Post" is a pre-fix that means "after," and "traumatic" is the adjectival form of "trauma." [90] "Trauma" is taken from a Greek word that means "wound," and in its adjectival form means "relating to wounds." One of the definitions for "stress" is "the deformation caused in a body" by an outside force, and "injury" means "an act that damages or hurts"[91] Thus, PTSI is the "hurt" caused by "the deformation" that came "after" there was a situation relating to "wounds."

The Heart

One of the organs "deformed" in someone with PTSI is the heart. Although the actual pathology has only recently been quantified, the "dis-ease" in the heart is not a new discovery. A rapid or fluttering heartbeat in soldiers suffering from warzone exposure was diagnosed by physicians in the Civil War as "irritable heart" or "trotting heart."[92] A rapid and irregular heartbeat is still one of the common attributes of

PTSI. [93] This wound to the normal working of the heart can progress to further debilities. "Chronic sympathetic arousal . . . may contribute to the progression of coronary heart disease through reduced heart rate variability; increased sympathetic and decreased parasympathetic activity are [sic] linked to ventricular arrhythmias and sudden death." [94] Further research may clarify the actual structures of the heart that are deformed by PTSI, but statistics already indicate that warriors who are at a place where bodies are wounded can have their hearts deformed by the experience. [95]

The Brain

Another part of the body that is "deformed" or contaminated by exposure to a warzone is the brain. The most common structural change related to PTSI occurs in the hippocampus and the amygdala. [96] The hippocampus is believed to control learning and memory. [97] Damage to the hippocampus affects short-term memory and interrupts the person's ability to integrate his or her new experiences into his or her belief system. [98] The hippocampus is also involved in telling the body to return to stasis following a stressful event. [99] PTSI caused by combat can reduce a person's hippocampus by 26 percent of its original volume. [100]

Besides the hippocampus, the amygdala can be damaged by warzone exposure. This cephalic member controls a person's response to fear. [101] A single event can cause permanent changes to the neurocircuitry of a person's amygdala. [102] A change in the neuro-pathways of a person's amygdala can elicit fear-responses from any component part of a stressful event (for example, similar sights, sounds or smells), which may no longer be an ingredient of a life-threatening situation. Such automatic, and often inappropriate, reactions may cause people with PTSI to no longer trust their perceptions of reality. [103] Currently, the only way to expunge a particular fear-conditioned reaction originating in the amygdala is to remove this part off the subject's brain. [104]

Other components of the brain can also be corrupted by PTSI. Some studies have noted a decrease in the activity of the thalamus which processes sensory information.[105] Other studies have shown a decrease in blood flow to the medial prefrontal cortex which can result in the failure of this part of the brain to function.[106] "[D]ecreased activation of the dorsal and rostral anterior cingulate and altered activation in the ventromedial prefrontal cortex, regions involved in experience and regulation of emotion, have repeatedly been observed in patients with PTSI."[107] Scholars admit that knowledge of the interaction between what a subject experiences and the physical ramifications, or "wounds," he or she incurs, especially relating to brain functioning, is still in its infancy.[108] Understanding the actual mechanism that converts a violent incident on the surface of the planet into the very cells of the human body is still beyond the realm of science.[109]

The Nephesh

Thus far, this chapter has demonstrated how warzone experiences can alter the physical functioning and structure of the heart and the brain. Once an alteration has occurred in the structure of sentient organs, it is difficult to delimit the impact on an individual's cognitive and conscious abilities. For materialist scholars, these structural changes are sufficient to explain the presence of PTSI. According to materialist theory a person's perception of reality and their behavior and reactions are driven by the physical processes and structure of their cardiac and/or cephalic region.[110] Even a non-materialist therapist is challenged to prove beyond all doubt where the physical limit of an injury ends and the non-physical begins. Because this study is written from a Christian perspective, it contains an *a priori* assumption that the physical body has a spiritual counterpart.[111] In regards to PTSI, one corollary that follows from this assumption is: If it is possible for the organs of the physical body to be altered by association with conflict, then the central components of an individual's spiritual corpus also can be 'deformed' or corrupted by exposure to a warzone environment. To avoid the disagreement in theological and secular circles about the boundaries of mind, soul and spirit, this study has chosen "nephesh" (נפש) to represent the non-material aspect of a human being. A classic Hebrew dictionary defined "nephesh" as "soul, self, life, creature, person, appetite, mind, living being, desire, emotion, passion."[112] In the First Covenant *nephesh* is a substitute word used to convey the very identity of a person.[113] The next section will catalogue some of the ways the nephesh is altered by war.

A common nephesh wound is "amputation." With this injury the nephesh of the warrior is unable to access, or is cut off from, a previous relationship or sometimes all relationships.[114] "A person may complain of feeling detached or estranged from other people . . . or that the ability to feel emotions . . . is markedly decreased."[115] This estrangement includes relationships with the soldier's children, spouse, parents, friends and even members of the soldier's unit.[116] The "amputation" is not only toward people: many times, the veteran feels cut off from God.[117] His or her nephesh is unable to connect God with the violence and arbitrary nature of the combat experienced.[118] "The pollution we accumulate through participation in war interrupts our connection to the Divine."[119]

Another common form of warzone contamination is guilt.[120] The best definition for this wound to the nephesh is, "feelings of culpability [especially] for imagined offenses or from a sense of inadequacy."[121] This "corruption" of the pre-war nephesh is particularly injurious to the veteran because of the culture established through military service. The motto "Duty, Honor, Country" used by the U.S. Military Academy at West Point helps illustrate the importance of character within martial culture. Jonathan Shay, a staff psychiatrist with the Department of Veterans Affairs, defined an army as "a moral construction."[122] Another group of clinical psychologists noted, "It is important to appreciate that the military culture fosters an intensely moral and ethical code of conduct . . . However, once redeployed and separated from the military culture and context . . . some service members may have difficulty accommodating various morally conflicting experiences."[123] Not only do service members feel guilty for violations of their own moral code, but they also sometimes condemn themselves for the simple act of returning home alive when others perished.[124] Guilt is one reason some veterans do not seek help for their stress injuries after returning from deployment.[125]

Depression is a very common wound found in the nephesh of war veterans. Most clinicians make a distinction between "depression" and PTSI, but Jonathan Shay notes that, "PTS[I] can unfortunately mimic virtually any condition in psychiatry."[126] Certainly this is true for depression and PTSI. These two maladies appear in veterans with such regularity that they are frequently grouped together in the literature of the Department of Veterans Affairs.[127] To be diagnosed with depression a person must "have a persistent constellation of symptoms, including depressed mood, inability to experience pleasure, or loss of interest in almost all activities, that occur almost every day for two weeks."[128] The author of Psalm 51 shows the presence of these symptoms when he asks God in verse eight, "Make me to hear joy and gladness; that the bones which You have broken may rejoice." (Ps 51:8) While these symptoms for depression can have a biological etiology,[129] there may also be cognitive explanations for these characteristics in an individual.[130] War introduces negative cognitions-- for example, the expectation of harm from every situation-- into the nephesh as a survival mechanism.[131] Other situations, like enemy camps disguised underground in pastoral settings, can cause a veteran to mistrust his or her perceptions.[132] These are only two of the many ways that information processing and the values associated with that information can become skewed by contact with the extreme environment of war. It is then easy to understand how the wound of depression can be found in a veteran, because a depressed person will "maintain . . . pain-inducing and self-defeating attitudes despite objective evidence of positive factors in his life."[133]

This review of the wounds to body and nephesh was not meant to be an exhaustive catalogue of every possible injury caused by PTSI. The purpose was to establish these "wounds" as deformations caused ". . . by the introduction of unwholesome or undesirable elements"[134] to his or her pre-conflict composition. If PTSI can be seen as "contamination", then this study suggests that the Church may have the means to "purify" the body and nephesh of the "wounded" veteran of their warzone injuries.

CHAPTER 3

Death-Shadow

Command the sons of Israel that they put out of the camp . .
. whoever is defiled by a dead body. (Nu 5:2)

You have crushed us in the place of jackals and covered us
with the shadow of death. (Ps 44:19)

Being around corpses and/or handling dead bodies is traumatic.[135]
Death and the possibility of death is also an emotional stressor.[136]
Modern psychiatrists list exposure to a deadly environment as the first
requirement for Posttraumatic Stress Injury (PTSI).[137] Ironically, many
people who survive a brush with death often feel cutoff from God
after their deliverance. Psychological studies have shown that, "One of
the most pervasive effects of traumatic exposure is the challenge that
people experience to their existential beliefs concerning the meaning
and purpose of life, particularly at risk is the strength of their religious
faith and the comfort that they derive from it."[138] This clinical
observation mirrors the reactions found in a family of ancient warriors.
These warriors are the Benim Korah (the sons of Korah) and their
trauma is captured in Psalm 44.

This particular psalm is labeled a *maskil* (מַשְׂכִּיל) which is "a
didactic [instructive] poem."[139] On the subject of PTSI this psalm has
much to teach the Church. Perhaps the premiere point of instruction
is the Hebrew name for traumatic stress injury which appears to be
צַלְמוּת, and is commonly translated "shadow of death" (Psalm 44:19).
This Hebrew word is actually a compound made up of צֵל (shadow)
and מוּת (death).[140] Some scholars define צַלְמוּת as "shelter of death"
and see the term as an epithet for a place where the dead reside.[141] The
hypothesis that צַלְמוּת is the "residence of the dead" invites an
examination of God's instructions to the living who enter a residence
with a dead body in it. The consequences are found in Numbers 19:

Those who touch a corpse and do not purify themselves
remain unclean . . . They defile the LORD's Tent, and they

will no longer be considered God's people. In the case of a person who dies in a tent, anyone who is in the tent at the time of death or who enters it becomes ritually unclean for seven days. Every jar and pot in the tent that has no lid on it also becomes unclean. If any touch a person who has been killed or has died a natural death outdoors or if any touch a human bone or a grave, they become unclean for seven days. (Nu 19:13-16 GNB)

As this Scripture illustrates, in the residence where a person dies, even the clay pots become contaminated with death. The Christian Scriptures express the "clay pot" concept metaphorically in the second letter to the Corinthians: " Yet we who have this spiritual treasure are like common clay pots . . . At all times we carry in our mortal bodies the death of Jesus" (2Co 4:7 & 10 GNB). The ability of another person's death to invade the "clay pot" of a living person is an undeniable principle in Scripture.

The diagnosis of PTSI was not even possible prior to 1980.[142] Scholars acknowledge that the disorder currently called PTSI has had many names through the history of war.[143] The Greek historian Herodotus, in the fifth century BCE, labeled one man with symptoms of warzone stress "the Trembler."[144] In the 1600's "Swiss Disease" was the name given to behavior many Swiss villagers showed after they were conscripted into foreign armies. When this malady was shown to affect other nationalities, it was renamed "nostalgia."[145] The first purely American moniker for battle-related nervous breakdown arose during the Civil War when doctors began diagnosing "soldier's heart." World War I veterans called this unseen plague "shell-shock", and the World War II generation labeled it "battle fatigue." Only after the Vietnam War did clinicians start calling the emotional and psychological injuries of combat Posttraumatic Stress [Injury].   William Nash, one of the foremost authorities on psychological injuries from the Global War on Terror, says, "Persistent reactions to combat and operational stress are clearly identifiable in the literature of antiquity."[146] Nash is referring to Jonathan Shay's work on Homer's *Iliad* and the *Odyssey*.[147] Even though Psalm 44 is more ancient than the works of Homer, Dr. Shay's analysis of the *Iliad* is an excellent resource to show the parallels between the "shadow of מות" and PTSI from a narrative perspective.

As Nash's comment on the presence of PTSI in the works of antiquity confirms, there is general agreement in the psychological community that Shay is accurate in his diagnosis of Achilles even though Homer never coined a word for the condition. Dr. Shay also has the confidence of the military community on this subject. In 1997 *Achilles in Vietnam* was named to the Marine Corps Professional Reading Program for all members of the U.S.M.C. Although as a psychiatrist with the V.A. Dr. Shay is intimately familiar with the *Diagnostic and Statistical Manual of Mental Disorders*, as an author he used five common features of Vietnam veterans' narratives to establish a complementary matrix for identifying PTSI in the ancient veteran Achilles.

Robert J. Lipton, who also worked with Vietnam veterans, recommends a "death-centered" focus for warzone trauma.[148] Lipton calls the core influence in PTSI the "death-imprint."[149] The alternative diagnostic scale Dr. Shay establishes in *Achilles in Vietnam* also has a death-imprint. Its five components form the first chapters of his book.[150] Each chapter has some factor dealing with death. In the first chapter there is "victory, defeat, and the hovering dead" to indicate how the meaning of death changes with the outcome of the war (p.6); chapter two deals with "respect for the dead" as an indicator of social relationships (p.29); chapter three describes Achilles grief as "being already dead" in his nephesh (p.51); chapter four looks at "deserving the death sentence" to describe survivor's guilt (p.72); and chapter five has a section on 'Revenge as reviving the dead' that addresses atrocities (p.89). Shay's alternative template will be referred to in this study as the "Achilles Matrix". This study has re-worked Shay's original sub-section descriptions in the Achilles Matrix to facilitate an analysis of Death-Shadow in Psalm 44. The subtitles for the five divisions of the Achilles Matrix are: 1) Dead Wrong; 2) Dead Space; 3) Living Dead; 4) Proxy Dead; 5) Walking Dead. The next section of this study will examine Psalm 44 for evidence of these five symptoms.

Dead Wrong

The trigger event for the Achilles Matrix is violation of *themis*.[151]

32

In *Achilles* "themis" is defined as "what's right."[152] Dr. Shay believes that PTSI for Achilles and Vietnam veterans began with a moral affront: "Any army, ancient or modern, is a social construction defined by shared expectations and values.. . When a leader destroys the legitimacy of the army's moral order by betraying "what's right," he inflicts manifold injuries on his men." [153] Another group of clinical psychologists noted, "It is important to appreciate that the military culture fosters an intensely moral and ethical code of conduct . . . . some service members may have difficulty accommodating various morally conflicting experiences."[154] Thus when a leader commits an offense that is "Dead Wrong", the leader introduces the first ingredient for PTSI into the warriors of his or her command. In *Achilles* Shay points to King Agamemnon's wrongful seizure of Achilles' *gera* or "prize of war" as the event that broke the social contract for Achilles and set in motion his subsequent self-destructive behavior.[155]

The journey to צלמות in Psalm 44 by the Benim Korah is also due to the betrayal by their leader. In their case it is God himself. These warriors draw God's attention to the fact, ". . . we have not forgotten You nor dealt falsely in Your covenant. Our heart is not turned back, nor have our steps turned aside from Your way" (Ps 44:17-1 8). The Benim Korah believe it is "dead wrong" that in return for their faithfulness God sold the Benim Korah to their enemies, scattered the Benim Korah among the Gentiles, made them retreat in battle and allowed the enemy to plunder the Benim Korah completely (Ps 44:10-12). The Benim Korah tell God that he never treated their ancestors like he is treating them (Ps 44:1-3).

Dead Space
    In Shay's analysis of *The Iliad*, the next step taken by an individual in the throes of PTSI is the "Shrinkage of the Social and Moral Horizon."[156] On the battlefield when units pull back from each other to secure their own perimeter, their consolidation creates "dead space", an area of no-man's land. The same is true when esprit de corps breaks down within a unit and everyone fends for themselves. Achilles begins the *Iliad* connected to the entire army, but after the indignity done to him by King Agamemnon, he withdraws to just " . . . his own troop, the Myrmidons."[157] In a modern parallel, one of the Vietnam veterans in *Achilles* commented that his loyalty shrank from his

battalion of 850, then to his company of seventy-two, and finally to just the five men of his reconnaissance team.[158] Everyone else was "dead" to this veteran.

The retreat of the social and ethical perimeter for the Benim Korah is not documented with the detail of the *Iliad* nor Shay's *Achilles,* but this phenomenon is still present. The "dead space" starts when the people who share the same village with the Benim Korah pull back from these veterans (v. 13). The next verse illustrates how shunning the Benim Korah has moved to the international stage (v.14). Even God has disassociated himself from the Israelite army in the minds of these veterans (v.9).

Living Dead

Shay mentions a phenomenon of PTSI that he labels "already dead".[159] He associates this reaction with extreme grief in the veteran at the loss of a "special friend." In the case of Achilles, the grief is the result of the death of his best friend Patroklos. Shay recognized that Homer illustrates Achilles' inner-state by use of the same funereal terms for both the dead Patroklos and the living Achilles.[160] In this stage of PTSI the veteran is still very much "alive" to emotional pain, but he or she cannot imagine life in the post-deployment world without their friend.[161]

The Benim Korah also express grief at the loss of their "special friend." They, like Homer, use language reminiscent of death. At verse 23 these veterans ask "Why do You sleep, O Jehovah? Arise! Do not cast *us* off forever." The Hebrew word for "sleep" in this verse is יָשֵׁן.

It can be a figure of speech for "death."[162] Job uses יָשֵׁן, as just such a euphemism when he expresses his desire to sleep because "[t]hen I would have been at rest with kings and wise men of the earth, who built ruins for themselves" (Job 3:13-14). Job has many of the same symptoms of PTSI as the Benim Korah. The Benim are reluctant to go to their "funeral" but they feel like the Living Dead, "Yea, for Your sake we are put to death all the day long; we are counted as sheep for the slaughter" (v.22). It is clear they wish their special friend were not "asleep."

34

Proxy Dead

This stage of the Achilles Matrix is for survivors' guilt. Some veterans believe they are alive by mistake.[163] As Dr. Nash notes "Not only do service members feel guilty for violations of their own moral code, but they also sometimes condemn themselves for the simple act of returning home alive when others perished.[164] Achilles always thought that it would be his friend Patroklos who would sail home to mentor the war-orphaned son of Achilles.[165] Since Achilles believes he failed Patroklos by not being present to take the fatal spear thrust from Hector, Achilles pronounces his own death-sentence and vows to not go home alive either.[166] Dr. Shay notes that guilt is a common reaction to surviving.[167]

A similar emotion is present in Psalm 44. The Benim Korah are always thinking about their כלמה (v.15). *Strong's Concordance* defines כלמה as "*disgrace:* - confusion, dishonor, reproach, shame."[168] This reaction is brought about because they are able to hear ". . . the voice of the enemy and avenger" (Ps 44:16). Lipton asserts that "Death Guilt" is the product of ". . . the limited capacity to respond to the threat and the self-blame for that inadequate response." Based on Lipton's thesis and the text of Psalm 44 the Benim Korah have a valid reason for guilt. These veterans may not have expected to be alive in the aftermath of God's departure from their ranks, especially since they are being sacrificed like sheep. The intensity of their military defeat is metaphorically depicted as being "crushed in the place of תנין . . ." (v.19). This word can mean "a marine or land *monster, that is, sea serpent* or *jackal:* - dragon, sea-monster, serpent, whale."[169] In the book of Job, God has advice for the veteran who tries to fight with a similar monster "Lay your hand on him, think of the battle; you will never do it again." (Job 41:8) Having survived this "crushing" the Benim describe their emotional state as ". . . covered . . .with the shadow of death" (v.19). More than any other aspect of Psalm 44, this use of "death-shadow" most closely resembles Lipton's requirements for "Death Imprint." Lipton believes, "The death imprint consists of the radical intrusion of an image feeling of threat or end of life."[170] The Psalmist's description of an attack by God, in a land associated with monsters, sounds like a radical intrusion of mortality. So it follows that the Benim Korah feel a "death imprint" or "death-shadow" after the event. Although there

35

is still one more stop on the journey to full PTSI the Benim Korah know that death has become part of their existence now.

Walking Dead

The final measurement of PTSI on the Achilles Matrix is the "Walking Dead." A person at this point of PTSI has progressed beyond emotional pain and now is unable to access most of their internal resources. Dr. Shay summarizes Achilles' psychic constitution at this stage as, "no prudence, ethics, piety, personal gain, compassion, fatigue, or physical pain, not the rational requirements of victory or fidelity to a dead friend" are within this Greek soldier's range.[171] Moving beyond the *Iliad*, Dr. Shay predicts a pattern for the veteran who has entered this fifth state, "[I]t imparts emotional deadness and vulnerability to explosive rage to his psychology and a permanent hyper arousal to his physiology—hallmarks of post-traumatic stress [injury] in combat veterans."[172]

A better metaphor than the "walking dead" for the Benim Korah at this juncture of their journey to PTSI might be "the crawling dead." Robert Lipton says, "The survivor undergoes a radical but temporary diminution in his or her sense of actuality in order to avoid losing this sense completely and permanently." At verse 25 they lament, "For our soul is bowed down to the dust; our belly holds fast to the earth." The Benim assume this position when it appears to them that God has forgotten the cost of their military reversals (v.24). These veterans recognize their inability to change their constitution, which may have been altered like the nephesh trauma imparted to the warriors in Vietnam. In this state the Benim Korah make a final plea for God to redeem them from a life in this altered condition (v.25).

God may have answered the prayers of the Benim Korah in some other temporal manner but the prophet Isaiah showcases God's final solution to the wound caused by death-shadow. The redeemer would start in Galilee by illuminating the lives of people who are stained with death-shadow (Isa 9:2)

Jesus And Death-Shadow

"The land of Zebulun and the land of Naphtali, *by* way of *the* sea, beyond Jordan, Galilee of the nations! The people who sat in darkness saw a great Light; and Light has sprung up to those who sat in *the* region and shadow of death." (Mt 4:15-17)

And when he had got out of the boat, straight away there came to him from the place of the dead a man with an unclean spirit. He was living in the place of the dead... And all the time, by day and by night, in the place of the dead, and in the mountains, he was crying out and cutting himself with stones... And Jesus said, What is your name? And he made answer, My name is Legion, because there are a great number of us. (Mk 5:2-9 BBE)

When Matthew's Gospel proclaimed Jesus as the "great Light" for the people who live in the "shadow of death", the author was quoting the prophecy of Isaiah. In this prophecy Isaiah predicts that the people in Galilee who are totally encompassed by צלמות (death-shadow) will be delivered of their problem. Matthew's Gospel lists this prophecy in chapter four and in chapter eight describes an example of Jesus performing the very acts promised by Isaiah. In Matthew 8:28 two Galileans, who live in a cemetery, are delivered of their צלמות. A longer form of this narrative is found in the Gospel of Mark.

The version of "The Gadarene Demoniac" found in Mark 5 is ". . . the longest, most detailed and literarily complex . . ." versions of this narrative in the Synoptic Gospels.[173] The Markan narrative is relevant to this portion of the study because the tomb-man may have been a veteran. Many aspects of this narrative have military undertones.[174] The tomb-man names his "contamination" using a foreign military designation (legion) rather than the many colloquial terms available to him.[175] The corresponding Hebrew military term for "legion" is "eleph" or "ribbo" (אלף or רבבה) depending on the size of the unit.[176] The frequency of these terms in the Hebrew Scripture demonstrates

37

that these terms were in common usage. An example of civilians using these military designations is found in the song the women sing for Saul and David, "Saul has slain his אלף, and David his רבבה" (1 Sa 18:7).

The name for the tomb-man is never revealed in Mark 5. It is those unclean spirits that controls his actions who are named as "Legion." For ease of use the tomb-man will be designated "Decapolitan" (a person from Decapolis) henceforth in this study. Agreement on whom or what was afflicting Decapolitan has proven impossible in modern Christendom. Although the text in Mark 5:2 says "an unclean spirit", the parallel narratives in Matthew and Luke say "demons" (Mt 8:28; Lk 8:27). Older commentaries on these parallel passages support both demonic possession and mental illness.[177] Even today, faithful Christians can see mental illness rather than "unclean spirit" in Decapolitan's story.[178] Perhaps an alternative explanation that might satisfy both literalists and modernists is to focus on Decapolitan as under the control of "the fear of death."

This phrase comes from Hebrews 2:15 but it also describes the chief characteristic of "Legion" which is concern with non-existence (Lk 8:31). In his commentary on *The Epistle to the Hebrews*, H.W. Montefiore captures the vagueness of the ontology of "the fear of death" in Hebrews 2:15, "It is not specified who enslaves men in this way".[179] What is known about the "fear of death" is that Jesus is able to ἀπαλλάσσω a person from its influence. This Greek word is usually translated as "deliver" but the first definition listed by *Strong's Concordance,* based on its component parts, is "to *change away.*" The key component word is ἀλλάσσω which means "to make different."[180] The author of Hebrews shows a consistent correlation throughout his epistle between "death" and "personal change."[181] Wherever people encounter "death", the author believes that a change in a person's nephesh situation is possible through Jesus.[182]

The secular guide for psychological diagnosis is the *Diagnostic and Statistical Manual IV Text Revised (DSM-IV-TR).* The Bible does not provide enough history about Decapolitan to check his behavior against the clinical standards set in the *DSM-IV-TR* and arrive at a conclusive diagnosis. However he matches many characteristics of Charles Marmar's and Mardi Horowitz's "Phase-Oriented Model of

Stress Response Syndromes" for people with PTSI.[183] Decapolitan also has anecdotal similarities with Vietnam veterans who provided narratives for *Achilles in Vietnam.*[184]

Marmar and Horowitz list five "Common Post-Stress Experiences and Their Pathological Intensifications."[185] Jesus displays no knowledge of Decapolitan's response to his initial trauma, but in the narrative of Mark 5, Decapolitan displays all five criteria in their pathological intensifications. The obvious one is "maladaptive avoidance-withdrawal" since Decapolitan is living and sleeping in a graveyard rather than with his family (Mk 5:2,3 and 19). Using stones to cut himself, Decapolitan demonstrates "physiological disruptions" (Mk 5:5). His "impaired social functions" are manifest not only by his living conditions, but by his inability to be controlled by any form of social and physical restraint (Mk 5:3-4). Jesus learns of Decapolitan's "panic and dissociative reactions" when Decapolitan is terrified that Jesus has come to hurt him, and then answers Jesus' inquiry about his identity with the statement, "We are many" (Mk 5:7-9). The final sign of injury after a traumatic event is "inability to go on with life." Even though Decapolitan is not from that part of Galilee, the unclean spirit begs Jesus to remain in that isolated area (Mk 5:10).

An earlier section of this study utilized the Achilles Matrix, an alternate scale for diagnosing PTSI based on Jonathan Shay's *Achilles in Vietnam,* to analyze the presence of PTSI/Death-shadow in Psalm 44. According to the Achilles Matrix, the last stage of PTSI is "The Walking Dead." Decapolitan in Mark 5 is described as a "man of tombs" which seems to be a synonym for the "walking dead." Shay listed the markers that would indicate someone is in the last stage of PTSI.[186] The ones that apply to Decapolitan are:

Beastlike	Godlike	Socially disconnected
Mad	Enraged	Devoid of fear
Reckless	Frenzied	Indiscriminate
Insensible to pain		
Inattentive to own safety		

The Markan text informs readers that Decapolitan is living in a cemetery, covered with scabs and dried blood from his own self-mutilation. "Trauma and personal loss, can lead a depressed person to think about hurting or killing themselves."[187] One scholar notes that the description of Decapolitan being heavily restrained "is more fitting of a wild beast than a human being (πεδαις και αλυσεσιν δεδέσθαι; v. 4)"[188]. Yet Decapolitan demonstrates god-like ability not only to break shackles and chains, but to recognize Jesus in his heavenly office as "Son of the Most High God" (Mk 5:7). Decapolitan's designation for Jesus is significantly higher than Peter's label for his leader. Three chapters later Peter could only declare that Jesus is "the Christ" (Mk 8:29).

The broken shackles were a reminder of Decapolitan's continuing social disconnection, while his constant crying out and self-inflicted injury points to madness and indiscriminate anger at himself and others. "Trauma can be connected with anger in many ways . . . intense feelings of anger and aggressive behavior can cause relationship . . . problems."[189] Rather than fearless, the spirit that drives Decapolitan is more suicidal. Here a cluster of symptoms- "indiscriminate", "reckless", "frenzied", "insensible to pain", "inattentive to own safety" are manifested by Decapolitan. He charges at Jesus knowing that Jesus can destroy him. When these unclean spirits leave Decapolitan and enter the pigs, the pigs manifest the same attraction for self-harm and commit mass suicide. Jonathan Shay notes that many Vietnam veterans chose suicide as a form of purification.[190] At the narrative's conclusion Decapolitan has been cleansed of his nephesh issues and is "in his right mind" (Mk 5:15). Ironically, for this veteran the "legion" was discharged from him rather than Decapolitan being discharged from the legion. As his name in this study indicates, he was able to return home.

The Benim Korah and Decapolitan were altered in their nephesh by exposure to death. The Scriptures names their affliction as "death-shadow" and their symptoms match the predicted categories in the Achilles Matrix and the Phase-Oriented Model of Stress Response Syndromes. Despite the years of experience and practical therapy that are the basis of these two complimentary paradigms of warzone stress trauma, neither the Achilles Matrix nor the Phase-Oriented Model of Stress Response Syndromes is a contender to replace the *Diagnostic and Statistical Manual IV-Text Revised (DSM-IV-TR)* as the therapeutic standard for diagnosing PTSI. Yet Psalm 44 and the narrative of Decapolitan in Mark 5 did not contain enough material to be scrutinized by this clinical standard. However, other passages in the Bible do contain enough relevant material to suggest a diagnosis using the guidelines in *DSM-IV-TR*. The next chapter will analyze other veterans in the Scriptures using this clinical standard to see whether the symptoms of death-shadow that they manifest are sufficient for a clinical diagnosis of PTSI.

CHAPTER 4

Biblical Warriors with PTSI

> PTSD is the second most commonly diagnosed psychiatric disorder. One cannot overestimate the degree to which trauma warps character. The most corrosive impact of horrific emotional trauma is to be found in the spiritual fabric of persons. The condition of PTSD is spiritual at its deepest level.
>
> (Bessel van der Kolk)[191]

There is a growing awareness that some of the patriarchs in the Bible show symptoms of PTSI. [192] Steven Luger, M.D., who is the medical director of the Hartford Medical Group, wrote an article entitled "Flood, Salt, and Sacrifice: Post Traumatic Stress Disorders in Genesis."[193] Dr. Lugar's premise is that Noah, Lot and Isaac suffered psychological injuries from the traumatic events contained in the Genesis narratives. At the Southern Baptist Convention's (SBC) 2009 Chaplaincy Development Conference, the conference workbook listed Job, David, Tamar, Jacob and Paul as person's with PTSI.[194]   It is significant that the SBC began their examination of PTSI with Job. The book of Job introduces the term "death-shadow" (צלמות) into Scripture. It occurs 18 times in the Hebrew canon and over half of these references are contained in the book of Job. The second person examined by the Chaplaincy workbook is David. His writings in Psalms are next to Job for usage of צלמות in Hebrew Scripture. This study maintains that צלמות is the Biblical term for PTSI.

Like Dr. Lugar's article, the SBC's workbook did not limit their Scriptural candidates to war-related PTSI, but included rape and incest among the types of situations that can lead to the onset of this injury. Although the SBC handbook listed Scripture narratives for use during breakout-sessions and a summary of the clinical requirements for PTSI, it did not include direct connection of symptoms with their Scriptural manifestations. In the section that follows, this study will attempt such a direct connection between the *Diagnostic and Statistical Manual of Mental Disorders IV* (*DSM-IV-TR*)[195] and the narratives where individuals are altered by their exposure to an environment of death.

TABLE 1	**Diagnostic Criterion A: Stressor**

The person has been exposed to a traumatic event in which both of the following have been present:

(1) The person has experienced, witnessed, or been confronted with an event or events that involve actual or threatened death or serious injury, or a threat to the physical integrity of oneself or others.

(2) The person's response involved intense fear, helplessness, or horror.

The *DSM-IV-TR*, published by the American Psychiatric Association, says the preeminent criteria to be diagnosed with PTSI is a person must have experienced, witnessed, or been confronted with an event or events that involve actual or threatened death (see Table 1).[196] This requirement is almost redundant in a study on warzone stress. Being a participant in war, with its concomitant risk of death and the mission to cause enemy death, is distressing to all who are subject to it. The Hebrew Scriptures list scores of people who were exposed to this risk. However, exposure to mortality is just the starting point for a warzone stress reaction. There are four more screening criteria that a veteran must meet before he or she can be diagnosed with PTSI. Because the Hebrew Scriptures were written to reveal God and not for the study of human foibles, there is often insufficient material about the reactions experienced by the person in a particular narrative. As a result only a limited number of persons are described in sufficient detail to hazard any diagnosis of their psychological condition. Of these main characters, this study has selected six individuals who were exposed to a death-contaminated environment and who had sufficient psychological reactions after the event to fit the other criteria for PTSI.

The first person to be examined is Lot. He was injured by death-shadow during the sacking of his city and his captivity as a Prisoner Of War (POW) of the Four Kings (Ge 14:9-12). After Lot, the other subjects are (in canonical order) Jacob, Samson, Saul, Elijah, and Job. Jacob was wounded by death-shadow at the slaughter of the people of Shechem (Ge 34:25). Samson's wound by death-shadow occurred when the Philistines burned his wife to death. (Jdg 15:6) Saul experienced death-exposure many times, but the wound of death-shadow was a souvenir from a battle with the Ammonites (1Sa 11:11). Elijah was injured by death-shadow as a result of Jezebel's soldiers murdering the prophets of Yahweh (1Ki 19:2). The final trauma victim is Job became a death-shadow casualty when he lost family and possessions to natural disasters and war (Job 1).

The person under scrutiny for PTSI regularly relives the emotional and physiological distress of the traumatic event. This can take several forms (see Table 2).

TABLE 2   **Diagnostic Criterion B: intrusive recollection**

B. The traumatic event is persistently re-experienced in one (or more) of the following ways:

(1) Recurrent and intrusive distressing recollections of the event, including images, thoughts, and perceptions (while awake).

(2) Recurrent distressing dreams of the event (nightmares).

(3) Acting or feeling as if the traumatic event were recurring (includes a sense of reliving the experience, illusions, hallucinations, and dissociative flashback episodes, including those that occur on awakening or when intoxicated).

(4) Intense psychological distress at exposure to internal or external cues that symbolize or resemble an aspect of the traumatic event.

TABLE 2   **(Continued)**

(5) Physiological reactivity at exposure to internal or external cues that symbolize or resemble an aspect of the traumatic event.

The form it took for Lot was, "intense psychological distress to events that symbolize or resemble an aspect of the traumatic event" (criterion B4). Lot had been in Sodom on the day its streets were not safe because raiders were ransacking the city. The streets had been where the survivors of Sodom were collected and where Lot took his first steps on the march to captivity. When the angels of Yahweh suggested to Lot that they intended to sleep in these same streets, he could not tolerate it and struggled to change their minds. As it says in the KJV, "he pressed upon them greatly" (Ge 19:3). The traditional explanation for this has been that Lot knew what would befall travelers caught in Sodom after dark.[197] This is based on speculation rather than the text. What is known from the scriptural record is that Lot had already experienced how insecure life in Sodom was, particularly for those not protected by any walls.

On the fateful night when the men of Sodom attempt to forcibly enter his house (like invading soldiers), it is not credible to think that Lot did not relive his earlier experience. One scholar comments that Lot's offer of his daughters to safeguard the angels is "fantastically disproportionate."[198] In a peacetime environment the sacrifice of a man's family legacy (Lot's remaining children) for two strangers would have been disproportional. Yet if Lot was reasoning from a warzone perspective, his response gains proportionality. It is merely an exchange of one set of captives for another (Ge 19:8).

Jacob associates Shechem with mortal danger (Ge 34:30). Years after the initial trauma, he discovers his ten sons are in the vicinity of this village, so he sends his most beloved child to check on their welfare (Ge 37:13). Although Joseph learns that his brothers are no longer at Shechem, Jacob never gets this information. As far as Jacob knows, the bloody clothes that are brought back to confirm Joseph's death are carried back from the site where his sons had previously murdered the local population. Just seeing Joseph's bloody garment is enough to send Jacob into a period of grief that is described in Scripture as long and intense. (Ge 37:34) In the chronology of the narrative, over two decades pass before Jacob appears again,[199] but when he does, it is clear he experiences "intense psychological distress at exposure to events that symbolize or resemble an aspect of the traumatic event" (criterion B-4). When his sons' return from Egypt without Simeon, Jacob flashes back to the day they came home without Joseph (Ge 42:36). When the continuing famine drives his children to consider a second trip to Egypt, Jacob again manifests his association of Egypt with the traumatic day at Shechem and experiences distress (Ge 43:14). Even after Jacob is reunited with Joseph, he continues to relive the day of slaughter at Shechem (Ge 48:22).

In Judges 15, the Hebrew Scriptures record that the Philistines burned Samson's wife and father-in-law to death. This is the tipping point for Samson, and his subsequent war with the Philistines grows out of this event. Every time he engages the Philistines it is a continuation of his response to the death of his wife (Jdg 15:7, 11). Something else happens when Samson engages the Philistines: the "Spirit of Yahweh" comes upon him. This phenomenon obscures the symptoms Samson displays that are caused by stress injury. One of these reactions is "sudden acting or feeling as if the traumatic event were recurring" (criterion B3). Delilah is aware of this stress reaction in Samson and uses it to test whether Samson has been honest with her. Four times she uses the phrase, "The Philistines are upon you!" (Jdg 16:9,12,14,20) to trigger Samson's association with his wife's death. Even though Samson does not have "Yahweh's Spirit" on the fourth occasion, the narrative says that Samson reacted in his usual way but without any power (Jdg 16:20). The story of Samson concludes with the final "acting out" by Samson. Once again surrounded by the people he associates with his wife's death, Samson declares, "Let me die with the Philistines!" and he collapses their temple on himself (Jdg 16:30), putting an end to those intrusive thoughts.

U.S. Army researchers have found that not all stress injuries are caused by a single event; they also can be triggered by long-term exposure to an environment of horror.[200] Although the Israelite women meant their song to honor Saul and his best fighter, the words "Saul has slain his thousands, and David his tens of thousands" expressed Saul's long-term exposure to mayhem and death. (1Sa 18:7) This song also makes Saul fear David as a rival: indeed, in the Hebrew Scriptures, there are no peaceful dynastic changes. David becomes the stressful event for Saul that represents a threat to his life and dynasty. Saul reacts with "intense psychological distress" (criterion B4) anytime David is prominent. This stress reaction is triggered in Saul by his daughter (1Sa 18:28--29), by his own tribesmen (1 Sam 22:8), and even by the rural priests in Israel (1Sa 22:17). Saul only gains freedom from his fears when he takes his own life at Mount Gilboa.

Following the slaughter of the other prophets, Elijah begins to experience "recurrent and intrusive distressing recollections" (criterion B1). Although the Scripture is silent about Elijah's mental state during his 40-day journey to Mount Horeb, the recurrent nature of the massacre in his thought-life is evident in Elijah's conversations with God. During his first audience with God, Elijah immediately brings up the traumatic event that brought him there. Even a hurricane, an earthquake and a firestorm fail to drive these thoughts from Elijah's mind, and he returns to this topic when he is granted his next audience with God (1Ki 19:14). One feature of his lament is his survival when the other members of his order perished. This biblical manifestation of "survivor's guilt" is an associated feature of PTSI, when the traumatic event is experienced by a group.[201] It is noteworthy that Elijah's "survivor's guilt" is the only aspect of his complaint that God dignifies with a response (1Ki 19:18). Earlier, Elisha had sought to end his suffering by theo-cide (1Ki 19:4). This is a form of assisted suicide in which God is the "weapon" the supplicant turns upon himself. Although Elijah is unsuccessful in this venture, the suicidal ideation this demonstrates will be important in subsequent analysis.

The book of Job provides the most complete examination of thought patterns in the wake of death found in the Hebrew Scriptures. The 34 chapters that are necessary for Job and his comforters to reach closure on his injury are testimony to the "persistence and intrusive nature" (criterion B1) of these thoughts in Job. Unique from the other PTSI candidates in this section, Job is the only one who experiences "recurrent distressing dreams" (Job 7:14), the second symptom of criterion B. Job also uses language in one rebuttal that indicates he might be experiencing "sudden acting or feeling as if the traumatic event were recurring" (criterion B3). In one response to Bildad, Job says that God is battering him with a whirlwind, a metaphor similar to the actual cause of his children's death (Job 9:17 ref. 1: 19). Twenty chapters later, Job is still describing his situation like the destruction caused by wind (Job 30:22). In Job's last rebuttal, he waxes nostalgically about the life he had before the attack, as he struggles to come to grips with his life in its aftermath.

TABLE 3   **Diagnostic Criterion C: avoidant/numbing**

C. Persistent avoidance of stimuli associated with the trauma and numbing of general responsiveness (not present before the trauma), as indicated by three (or more) of the following:

(1) Efforts to avoid thoughts, feelings, or conversations associated with the trauma.

(2) Efforts to avoid activities, places, or people that arouse recollections of the trauma.

(3) Inability to recall an important aspect of the trauma.

(4) Markedly diminished interest or participation in significant activities.

(5) Feeling of detachment or estrangement from others.

(6) Restricted range of affect (e.g., unable to have loving feelings).

(7) Sense of a foreshortened future (e.g., does not expect to have a career, marriage, children, or normal life span).

Criterion C requires the patient to exhibit three of seven avoidance behaviors. Because the Hebrew Scripture was written as a theological document, rather than a psychological treatise, it is difficult to find sufficient information about the characters' psyches in order to determine whether they meet three of these standards.

The Genesis account of Lot is a perfect example of insufficient data. The Hebrew Scripture only records four of his utterances, although he was part of Abraham's life for several decades. Yet one of those speeches is a plea to the angel of God to be allowed to live in the town of Zoar instead of the mountains where the angels want Lot to live. Given that Lot made this request (which was granted) it is significant that he voluntarily leaves Zoar to live in the very mountains he had earlier rejected. To understand why Lot cannot live in Zoar, the Hebrew Scriptures point out that this settlement was not always called Zoar. The town was originally named Bela (Ge 14: 2), and its people were defeated along with the people of Sodom during the invasion when Lot was taken prisoner. Lot may have mingled with the citizens of Bela during his captivity. After the destruction of Sodom, the renewed association with his earlier trauma might have proved too much for Lot. The narrative only says he feared to live in Zoar (Ge 19:30). It is this fear that drives Lot to a mountain cave, which would be an effective way to avoid any situation or activity that might remind him of what happened (criterion C2). Unfortunately, after he takes up residence there, he never utters another word in Scripture.

It is left to Lot's eldest daughter to display the rest of the symptoms for criterion C. Family members are also part of the PTSI experience.[202] Lot's daughter demonstrates a "feeling of detachment or estrangement from others" (criterion C5), and a "sense of a fore-shortened future" (criterion C7), as she convinces her sister to sleep with their father because no man will ever have a relationship with them (Ge 19:31--32). The technique she uses to overcome Lot's inhibitions is to intoxicate him with wine. The Hebrew Scriptures record Lot drank to the point where he did not know that a daughter had entered or left his bed (Ge 19:33). His eldest daughter's awareness that her father was capable of this level of intoxication suggests that he probably demonstrated this behavior on previous occasions. Such extreme self-medication can also be a way to avoid thoughts associated with a trauma.[203]

Some avoidance techniques are less subtle than others. This is the case with Jacob. He and his ten sons talk openly about the event that caused Jacob's neurosis, though from different perspectives (Ge 42:21,36). Jacob is not afraid to name the reason that he will not allow his youngest son Benjamin to accompany his brothers to Egypt. He states that he wishes to avoid a repeat of the tragedy that robbed him of his favorite son, Joseph (criterion C2). Jacob has other symptoms of criterion C. He displays a foreshortened future (criterion C7), as he declares that if Benjamin does not return, it will kill him (Ge 42:38). A third symptom requires more speculation because the Hebrew Scriptures do not comment on it, and like the case with Lot's daughters, the trauma is manifested in Jacob's children. They show "markedly diminished interest in significant activities" (criterion C4). One such significant activity is finding food for their families. They have to be driven by their father to do this. At one point he even asks them, "Why do you just keep looking at each other?" (Ge 42:1). Both times the sons travel to Egypt, it is at the initiative of their father, who appears to be the only one concerned with the survival of the clan (Ge 43:2).

Samson does not display clear symptoms of criterion C, according to the text of the Hebrew Scriptures. The Scripture provides no dialogue or direct attribution that Samson avoids anything connected to his tragedy, yet the text does contain some intriguing incongruities. Samson continues to be drawn to Philistine women (this is attributed to God [Jdg 14:4]), but he has relationships only with emancipated women. These are women, like prostitutes, who are not under the authority of their father. Their status is in contrast to that of his deceased wife, who lived and died with her father. Samson had a connection with his father-in-law, and this man was the last member of the family Samson spoke to before his family members were killed. By choosing women who were estranged from their fathers, perhaps Samson was seeking to avoid a situation similar to the one he experienced with his wife.

The Scripture only tells us that Samson's wife and her father were burned to death but not what technique was used. If the Philistines locked them in their house before setting it on fire,[204] then Samson's behavior at Gaza (Jdg 16:3) begins to resemble an avoidance technique (criterion C2). Finding himself similarly besieged, Samson removes not only the gate that impedes his escape, but all the other combustible material associated with it, the bar and gateposts. If escape had been Samson's only concern, there would have been no need for all this material to be removed, nor would he have needed to carry it such a considerable distance away from the situation. These extremes are what make Samson's behavior appear like a stress reaction. Another criterion C symptom demonstrated by Samson is that, on two occasions, Samson expresses a sense of a foreshortened future (criterion C7). When Delilah pesters him for the answer to her question, an act reminiscent of his wife, one translator renders Judges 16:16 as, "and his life was shortened to die."[205] Samson acts on his sense of a foreshortened future in the deed that ends this narrative (Jdg 16:30).

Saul lost his dynasty and his favor with God because of choices he made on the battlefield (1Sa 15:28). His enemies, his people, and even Saul himself associated David with those battlefields. It follows that if Saul wished to avoid these associations (criterion C1), he would also have to avoid David. Saul's preferred avoidance technique towards David was assassination. He tried to kill David himself (1Sa 18:11), he increased David's exposure to enemy forces (1Sa 18:17), and he even ordered his family or courtiers to strike the blow (1Sa 19:1). It is because of his fixation on David and what he represents that Saul becomes estranged not only from David but also from other significant people in his life (criterion C 5). Saul feels betrayed by both his daughter Michal (1Sa 19:17) and his son Jonathan (1Sa 20:30). Saul even feels detached from his fellow tribesmen (1Sa 22: 8). The third symptom that Saul displays of criterion C is a sense of a foreshortened future (C7). The very last time Saul encounters David, he confesses his conviction that David will survive him and he asks David not to kill his children after he is dead (1Sa 24:22).

Many modern commentators believe the prophet Elijah suffered from depression.[206] This is the most common mood disorder associated with PTSI.[207] Two of the symptoms of depression are poor appetite and hypersomnia, and the Angel of the Lord ministers to both these symptoms (1Ki 19:5--8) before allowing Elijah to walk for 40 days and nights into the desert. This trek may also be evidence of PTSI. It allowed Elijah the means to avoid people and situations that reminded him of the traumatic event (criterion C2). Elijah's detachment from others, including the separation from his servant at Beer-Sheba, is also symptomatic of a stress injury (criterion C5). He continues this behavior until the end of his life. Three times he tries to abandon the prophet Elisha after they have just conducted ministry. (2Ki 2:1,4,6). At Horeb, Elijah verbalizes his alienation from his fellow countrymen in both of his audiences with God (1Ki 19:10,14). In these same verses he also displays his sense of a foreshortened future (criterion C7). In Elijah's mind, there is a very real danger that the perpetrators of the earlier massacre will find him and finish their task.

Job displayed many behaviors that are consistent with criterion C. He had a markedly diminished interest in significant activities (criterion C4). He found all food tasteless and did not want to eat (Job 6:6-7). Job felt detached from his friends (criterion C5). He said they treated him like a moocher and he accused them of abandonment (Job 6:20-22). He accused them of laughing at his situation (Job 12: 4). Job sought their sympathy partially because he has a foreshortened sense of his future (criterion C7). He had lost all expectation that anything good would ever happen to him and believed that his life was at an end (Job 17:1). After the trauma, Job held a low opinion of life in general and felt it was short and pointless (Job 14:1-2,10). The only symptoms of criterion C that Job did not have were the first two, which deal with avoidance. Job seems to revel in reliving his trauma.

TABLE 4	**Diagnostic Criterion D: hyper-arousal**

D. Persistent symptoms of increased arousal (not present before the trauma), as indicated by two (or more) of the following:

    (1) Difficulty falling or staying asleep

    (2) Irritability or outbursts of anger

    (3) Difficulty concentrating

    (4) Hypervigilance (preoccupied with safety, a big one)

    (5) Exaggerated startle response

Criterion D focuses on over-activity of survival systems. Two different manifestations must be present to meet the standards for PTSI. The Hebrew Scriptures provide insufficient data to determine whether increased arousal was present in the cases of Lot and Jacob. According to the scriptural record, Saul had only one symptom of hyper-arousal and that will be addressed in the paragraph on symptom two. The three men who meet the full standard of criterion D are Samson, Elijah and Job.

The first symptom of excessive arousal from PTSI is an inability to fall asleep or stay asleep. Samson appears to have trouble staying asleep after his wife was killed. This was manifested first when he woke up at midnight while spending the night with the prostitute in Gaza (Jdg 16:3). Delilah knew that sleep was difficult for Samson, and that he would automatically come on guard when he woke up. Delilah's knowledge of Samson's reflex actions helps to explain why she used the phrase, "The Philistines are upon you!" to assess whether he had told her the truth about his strength (Jdg 16:9,12,14,20). In contrast, Job experienced visions and dreams that made it difficult for him to sleep (Job 7:13). Since Job did not mention the content of these dreams, it is difficult to determine if these visions are related to his ordeal. Job told his friends that sleep was an effort for him and brought him no rest (Job 7:4).

After inability to sleep, the next measure of hyper-arousal is whether the subject has outbursts of anger or pervasive irritability that were not present before his or her stress injury. "In more severe forms, particularly in cases which the survivor has actually committed acts of violence (as in war veterans), the fear is conscious and pervasive, and the reduced capacity for modulation may express itself in unpredictable explosions of aggressive behavior or in inability to express angry feelings."[208] Samson definitely had outbursts of anger and irritability (Jdg 14:9; 15:3,7; 16:28). Two of these predate his traumatic episode (Jdg 14:9; 15:3). The final two episodes were directly connected with the traumatic events in his life. Similarly Saul had an outburst of anger prior to his stress injury (1Sa 11: 6). This outburst included Saul killing and dismembering an ox and using its bloody quarters to threaten the populace of Israel. Against that backdrop it is nearly impossible to infer that Saul's anger issues were a result of a traumatic experience.

Two individuals from this study's control group display anger only after their ordeal. These are Elijah and Job. Elijah had a major outburst after Mount Carmel. He had the people capture the priests of Baal, but he was the one who killed all 450 of them (1Ki 18:40). Job was not as physical in his anger. Each time his friends tried to counsel Job, he responded with irritation and angry words. He called them, "miserable comforters" (Job 16:2). Job accused them of being "parasites" (Job 19:22). He said their counsel was as reliable as a mirage (Job 6:20). Job's anger was present in every discourse he engaged in from the times of his illness until God challenged him.

While Saul's preoccupation with David demonstrated concern for his own safety, it is difficult to judge if this was pathological or not, given that people were actually encouraging David to kill Saul (1Sa 26:8). Elijah also had a death threat against him, so the line between caution and injury is difficult to determine absolutely. The aspect that makes Elijah's response seem excessive is his isolation and his mental state. Elijah abandoned his servant and headed off into the desert alone (1Ki 19:3-4). He journeys forty days into total solitude. When he does speak to God, even with the geographic buffer he has put between himself and his executioner, he still is mentally focused on the threat to his life (1Ki 19:10).

TABLE 5	**Diagnostic Criterion E: duration**
E. Duration of the disturbance (symptoms in Criteria B, C, and D) is more than one month.	

Every one of the subjects meets criterion E. The timeline for the manifestation of Lot's symptoms started from the night before the destruction of Sodom and continued until the birth of his grandchildren when he was no longer mentioned in Scripture. Jacob exhibited his symptoms over a 20 year time span. Samson also had a 20 year reign as judge over Israel in conjunction with his symptoms. Saul pursued David through many seasons and campaigns. Elijah took at least 40 days to have his encounter with God. Job suffered the loss of his family and property after Satan attended an audience with God. When this did not cause Job to curse God, Satan returned after an undisclosed period of time, to ask that Job's body be tested. Only when this becomes known to his friends do they journey from their home country. When they see Job, they sit seven days before speaking to him. The time between the two tests and the friends' journey plus seven days of waiting is probably a period greater than one month.

TABLE 6	**Diagnostic Criterion F: functional significance**
F. The disturbance causes clinically significant distress or impairment in social, occupational, or other important areas of functioning.	

Criterion F requires a clinical level of impairment which is hard to determine from just a narrative. The trauma Lot experienced made it impossible for him to function among people who had shared his POW experience (Ge 19:30). To relieve his symptoms his chose to live in a cave. He also lost the ability to function in a healthy way with his daughters (Ge 19:33-35).

Jacob had significant issues with his sons following the slaughter at Shechem (Ge 34:27-30). Joseph, born after the slaughter and therefore not connected to their guilt, became the focus of Jacob's attention. Jacob indulged Joseph in ways not granted to his brothers (Ge 37:4 & 11). When Jacob thought his older sons were again at Shechem, Joseph was given the job of inspecting the welfare of his older brothers (Ge 37:14). Jacob's unbalanced relationship with his sons was at the root of the older brothers selling Joseph into slavery and dividing the family for decades (Ge 37:31-36).

Like Jacob, Samson's injury affected his functioning in a family setting. Samson did not seek the normal family obligations of a Jewish man after the murder of his wife and her family. He only sought illicit relationships (Jdg 16:1 and 4). Samson is the perpetual social outsider in each pericope of his adult life. As far as the narrative gives evidence, Samson was only reconnected with his extended family after his death (Jdg 16:31).

Saul's stress injury greatly affected his occupation. As king of Israel, Saul was responsible for the security of the nation. Due to the reactions Saul had any time he was with David, Saul drove out his most successful general and made his nation vulnerable to military defeat (1Sa 31:1-2). This military defeat also insured that the Kishite dynasty ended with Saul's last heartbeat.

Elijah and Job manifested similar occupational dysfunctions after their traumatic injury. Elijah abandoned his office as prophet of Yahweh, even though he had eliminated the competition from the priests of Baal (1Ki 18:40). Elijah was unable to continue as a prophet and God had to replace him with Elisha (1Ki 19:16). Job lost most, if not all, of his assets in the traumatic event. In its aftermath he was impaired occupationally and personally. He does not conduct his occupation during the entire period of Satan's trial of Job's character. His relationship with his wife and friends suffered (Job 2:10; 6:14-15). His extended family does not reconnect with him until he is functioning again (Job 42:11).

After this review of the six criteria for PTSI and the analysis of narrative information on these six veterans of the Hebrew Scriptures, readers are free to draw their own conclusions as to whether these men had clinical PTSI. What is beyond dispute is that these warriors were adulterated by their encounter with death. Clinical psychologists Brett Moore and Greg Reger believe, "The cognitive shift that occurs with being faced with one's own mortality and the realization that he or she may never see their family again can have a tremendous impact on the person."[209] The "tremendous impact" on these Scriptural veterans was that they became overshadowed by death. Samson and Saul became so focused on death that when confronted by a crisis, each took his own life. Elijah, Jacob, and Job longed to be dead but never took any action. Lot chose to live in a mountain cave that may have had more in common with a tomb than with a house.

Long before these men became overshadowed by death they were chosen by God to participate in the sacred story of His people. All of these men had, at least once in their life, an epiphany. Yet each came under the influence of death and there is no evidence that it was ever purged from their life. The next section of this study will look at the ministries that were practiced in the Scriptures to see if the people of God were ever given a way to cleanse death-shadow from their earthly lives.

CHAPTER 5

Veterans Ministries Past And Present

> When Abram came back from his victory over Chedorlaomer and the other kings, the king of Sodom went out to meet him in Shaveh Valley (also called King's Valley). And Melchizedek, who was king of Salem and also a priest of the Most High God, brought bread and wine to Abram, blessed him, and said, "May the Most High God, who made heaven and earth, bless Abram! (Ge 14:17-19 GNB)

The Bible reveals that people of faith have ministered to warriors since the earliest of times. When Melchizedek blessed Abraham in the Shaveh Valley he is the first person in Scripture to meet veterans returning from battle (Ge 14:17-18). Melchizedek's ministry to returning warriors is also featured prominently in the Epistle to the Hebrews in the Christian canon. Particularly at Hebrews 7:4-5 the superiority of Jesus' priesthood is established by the tithe of war-booty from Abraham to Melchizedek. Included among those returning warriors in the Shaveh valley was Lot, Abraham's nephew. The previous chapter of this study suggested that Lot developed symptoms similar to PTSI. This section will show that Lot did not receive the ministry best suited to this injury.

Although Melchizedek models one type of ministry in Scripture's original encounter between a servant of God and warriors, people of faith have tried a range of techniques since that time to provide succor to their veterans. Their efforts have encompassed the complete cycle of a warrior's deployment. Starting with pre-deployment intercessions and culminating with the internment of mortal remains, the Scriptures illustrate twelve categories of ministry provided to veterans. Sometimes the care of the soul was provided by another military member, sometimes by civilians, and sometimes by the religious communities. In this study the name given to each category was chosen to objectify what the people of God hoped to accomplish through their prayers and actions. These ministries are:

1) Ark	2) Holocaust	3) Shield	4) Compass
5) Bandage	6) Caisson	7) Exit	8) Canteen
9) Tambourine	10) Tablet	11) Souvenir	12) Wash

Each "model" or ministry is conducted in at least one narrative in Scripture, and some narratives contain multiple types of ministry within their story. Immediately after the narrative example(s) for a Scriptural ministry are set forth, this study will list modern forms of those ministries still practiced by Christendom in the 21st century.

Ark Ministry

During the time when God chose for himself an earthly locus above the cherubim on the ark of the covenant (Ex 25:22), the Israelites used the ability to transport God's presence onto the battlefield to minister to their armed forces. This portable "location" for God was the essence of the Ark ministry. Even the enemies of God's people acknowledged that having God physically present in the Israelite camp was a tremendous boost to morale (1Sa 4:7) The Scripture shows that sometimes God directed this ministry to be included in a military campaign and at other times the Israelites presumed upon the power of the Ark.

The Ark ministry is unveiled in Joshua 3 when Joshua told the Israelites "By this you shall know that the living God *is* among you, and He will without fail drive out from before you the Canaanites, and the Hittites, and the Hivites, and the Perizzites, and the Girgashites, and the Amorites, and the Jebusites. Behold, the ark of the covenant of the Lord of all the earth passes over before you into Jordan" (Jos 3:10-11). This ministry allowed 40,000 warriors to cross the Jordan River without getting their feet wet (Jos 4:13). The Ark ministry continued to be a critical feature of the Israelite military during the campaign to conquer Jericho. Every day the army followed the ark until Jericho was theirs (Jos 6:2-16). A different form of Ark ministry was demonstrated after the destruction of Ai. Instead of leading the army, the tribes gathered around the Ark according to the example Moses taught them for the institution of the law (Jos 8:33). The Ark ministry was then complemented by the Tablet Ministry (to be illustrated later).

During an invasion by the Philistines when Israel was still under the leadership of the judges, the people of ancient Israel re-instituted the Ark ministry. The Ark was brought into the military camp and the troops yelled so loud that the Philistines were convinced they would lose the coming battle (1Sa 4:6-7). In this instance the presence of the Ark did not guarantee victory for the Israelite warriors and many were killed and the rest were scattered (1Sa 4:10) The Ark itself was captured and never again was the presence of the Ark used as an encouragement to the veterans of Israel. On a personal level King Hezekiah invoked the Ark in his prayer to God that resulted in a military victory over the Assyrian army (Isa 37:16).

Speculation abounds as to the location of the Ark of the Covenant but if anyone actually knows its location it is a closely guarded secret. The last mention of the Ark in the Hebrew Scriptures is a prophecy that says ". . . in those days, says Jehovah, they shall say no more, The ark of the covenant of Jehovah! Nor shall it come to mind; nor shall they remember it; nor shall they visit *it*; nor shall it be made any more (Jer 3:16)." It would appear that time has come and Ark ministry is concluded according to the word of God.

Holocaust Ministry

Derived from the Greek word ὁλοκαύτωμα used in the LXX to describe the "whole burnt-offering" offered by Samuel for the army of Israel (1Sa 7:9), Holocaust ministry was intended to seek God's favor for the warriors of Israel. In the case of Samuel's participation in this vocation, successful results were seen. The same cannot be said when Saul practiced Holocaust ministry. Saul recognized that his soldiers were leaving because no one had initiated a holocaust on their behalf, so he did what he thought was required (1Sa 13:8-9). The Israelite warriors were not defeated when they fought the Philistines after Saul's misguided ministry, but Saul's time as their leader was greatly shortened because of his attempt to offer a holocaust(1Sa 13:14). Saul's final attempt at Holocaust ministry not only was fatal to his career as king but led to the destruction of his army (1Sa 15:26; 1Sa 31:6-7).

According to the Hebrew Scriptures the Holocaust ministry

required authorized celebrants. Saul learned to his peril that God is very particular who brings an offering by fire (1Sa 13:14; 1Sa 15:22; Lev 10:1). According to Exodus 29, the persons who are authorized to conduct Holocaust ministry have to be ordained at the Tabernacle (Ex 29:4). This location was later changed to the Temple (1Ki 8:4-8). When the Temple was destroyed by Titus, the ability to consecrate Levitical priests was lost.[210] For Jewish veterans the Holocaust ministry might be possible if a new Temple was built in Israel, but for Christians, even a new Temple would not make it possible to participate in Holocaust ministry again. That act has been completed once and for all (Heb 9:26).

Shield Ministry

This type of ministry derives its name from the Hebrew word מָגֵן used by Melchizedek in his blessing of the veterans (Ge 14:20). *Strong's* defines מָגֵן as "properly to *shield*; figuratively to *rescue*, to *hand* safely *over* (that is, *surrender*): - deliver."[211] Throughout the rest of this study, any occasion or ministry that asks for deliverance or acknowledges God's protection of military forces will be called a Shield ministry. In Genesis 14:20 Melchizedek blesses God Most High for "מָגֵן-ing" Abraham and his forces from their opponents. After Melchizedek used this word to minister to Abraham, God confirmed the shield ministry principle the very next time He and Abraham speak to each other (Ge 15:1).

The fact that Melchizedek was the initiator of ministry to veterans is often overlooked by scholars who study the encounter recorded in Genesis 14:18-20. The focus tends to be on Abraham as patriarch rather than military leader. This study will attempt to correct this deficiency for the sake of veterans. In this way warriors can see God's plan for them in the other Scriptural promises that are attached to the ministry of Melchizedek in Psalm 110 and the Epistle to the Hebrews. It is through the illumination of these later verses, particularly in the fifth chapter of Hebrews, that the Shield ministry of Melchizedek gains its full stature. T.K. Thomas notes:

> In a sense the writer puts all priests in their place - all Jewish priests and, proleptically, all their Christian successors: popes, cardinals, archbishops, metropolitans, bishops and priests

high and low, all who celebrate sacraments, preach the word, mediate, intercede and perform a variety of pastoral functions.. . The permanent priesthood of Jesus "in the order of Melchizedek" involves the abrogation of the old law, guaranteeing, as it does, a better covenant. And it means that Christ is able, through his unending priesthood, "to save completely those who come to God through him, because he always lives to intercede for them."[212]

There can be no denying that the persons who received Melchizedek's ministry were veterans and captives who had been exposed to death and destruction. (Ge 14:17) Melchizedek becomes the warriors' agent to acknowledge God's part in shielding the warriors from mortal injury. But Melchizedek also is the agent of God, and through his blessing, imparts "shielding" to the returning warriors from moral injury. Modern psychologists acknowledge there is a direct connection between moral injury and PTSI. [213] The translation of Melchizedek's name is "King of Righteousness" (Heb 7:2). He holds this office as Jesus' precursor (Heb 7:15). Melchizedek bestows this righteousness to those assembled before him. Evidence suggesting this impartation of righteousness is found in 2 Peter 2:7 where the Bible describes Lot as "righteous" despite his continued dwelling in Sodom. No other source of righteousness for Lot can be found in Scripture. This endorsement by the priest who is "King of Righteousness" on warriors who were "return[ing] from the slaughter"[214] is a necessary part of God's plan for re-integration into both human and divine fellowship.

The Hebrew word at the root of Shield ministry also means "to hand safely over."[215] This is the type of Shield ministry Moses established on high ground at the first battle against the Amalekites (Ex 17:9). As long as he kept his hands above his head "shielding" the army, his warriors had the advantage over the enemy. When his hands collapsed, the battle went badly for the army of Israel. When Moses appeared unable to sustain this shielding Aaron and Hur had Moses sit on a boulder. In this posture it was easier for them to help Moses' keep the army's spiritual "shield" in place (Ex 17:12).

Joshua, the general who was supported by the Shield ministry of

Moses, inherited this ministry when he was the leader of Israel. Joshua "shielded" the army during the conquest of Ai. At this battle, Joshua used his spear as a shield to give divine advantage to the soldiers in his army. (Jos 8:18) He did not take down this "shield" until the city was a heap of ruins (Jos 8:26). With the end of hostilities Joshua transitioned into other ministries for his warriors.

Using a different form of the Shield ministry, the father-and-son team of Obed and Azariah ministered to veterans of the Cushite campaign as they returned to Jerusalem in a much later period (2Ch 15:1-8). These prophets reminded King Asa about the military vulnerability during the time when judges ruled Israel. Obed recounted to the king how God shielded the people when they returned to him. In response to this sermon, Asa ordered the removal of foreign idols from the land and had the people gather to offer sacrifices to Yahweh (2Ch 15:10-11). The veterans themselves responded to the Shield ministry by giving a portion their booty, just like the returning warrior Abraham in the Shaveh valley. The effect of this Shield ministry was a long period of peace when the military was not exposed to war for twenty five years (2Ch 15:19).

The Hebrew Scriptures contain accounts of Shield ministry that are conducted prior to the troops deploying to war. The first is in 2 Chronicles 13 where Abijah, the king of Judah, reminded Jeroboam, the king of Israel, of the power of Yahweh to protect His followers. Abijah cited the intercessions and sacrifices that his priests had already made on behalf of his army (2Ch 13:12). This ministry allowed Abijah's warriors to be shielded from the ambush Jeroboam set for them (2Ch 13:14). The next instance of pre-deployment Shield ministry is in 2 Chronicles 20:1-30 where King Jehoshaphat initiated a national fast and a period of prayer before his forces leave for battle. The focus of the ministry was to seek God's intervention against their enemies. During the service the Spirit of God fell on a Levite who told the warriors that Yahweh would be the one fighting this battle for them (2Ch 20:17). After the battle is over and the booty has been gathered, the Judeans assembled to conduct a thanksgiving service for their safety before marching back to Jerusalem. (2Ch 20:26) The result of this ministry was that Judah's enemies came to believe that Yahweh is a member of Jehoshaphat's army.

The Christian Scriptures contain only a single instance of armed combat. This is the swordfight in the Garden of Gethsemane that precedes Jesus' arrest. The altercation is chronicled in all four Gospels.[216] Jesus' action towards friend and foe alike defines the essence of Shield ministry. Jesus "shielded" his disciples from the soldiers when he said, "I have told you that I AM. Therefore if you seek Me, let these go away; (that the word might be fulfilled which He spoke, "*Of* those whom You have given Me, I have lost not one of them")" (Jn 18:8-9). Jesus "shielded" the high priest's soldiers from Peter's sword and God's host in heaven when he said, "Put up your sword again into its place; for all who take *the* sword shall perish with a sword. Do you think that I cannot now pray to My Father, and He shall presently give Me more than twelve legions of angels?" (Mt 26:52-53). Jesus also instructed the officers on the needless risk they took in choosing this particular battlefield since he spoke daily at the temple (Mt 26:55; Mk 14:49; Lk 22:53). This counsel, if applied, would shield the soldiers from needless casualties in future engagements.

One other example of Shield ministry to military personnel is present in the New Testament among Jesus' disciples. On his journey to Rome, the apostle Paul was put under the authority of a centurion named Julius (Ac 27:1). However, it was Julius and his soldiers who find themselves under the authority of Paul before the end of their trip. This transition happened when Paul became their "shield" from the consequences of Julius' decision to ignore his advice. During the seaborne leg of the journey to Rome their ship encounters a fierce storm. After days of darkness, an angel informed Paul that he must speak before Caesar (Ac 27:24). The angel also told Paul that because of this vocation he will survive the storm and, as a gift, God would also hand over or "shield"[217] the soldiers and crew of the ship (Ac 27:24). Julius responded to Paul's ministry by preventing his soldiers from executing the prisoners to prevent escape (Ac 27:43). This narrative is the ultimate military ministry in the Christian canon. No more mention of veterans or deployments is made again until the battles of Armageddon (Rev 16:16)

Seeking protection for warriors before they depart to a combat zone, or thanking God for their safe return, is arguably the most common form of veterans' ministry in Christendom today. Individual believers perform this ministry informally every time they pray for a service member. Some churches incorporate intercession for the safety of veterans among congregational prayers in an informal manner, while other churches and their parent organization have intentionally included the security of the military into a formal part of their liturgy. There is little substantive difference between these acts by modern Christians and the Shield services conducted by the ancient Israelites. The primary principle of this ministry is to entreat God for his protection when the warriors are deploying and to thank him for his protection when they have returned. Here is a sampling of Shield rites:

United Methodist Church
Almighty God, we commend to your love and care, _____ . (Full Name) Be with him/her now as he/she prepares to face the challenges of deployment and the uncertainties of war. Grant him/her wisdom and courage so that he/she may discharge his/her duties with integrity and faithfulness. Help him/her to endure hardship with grace and humor. Fill him/her with compassion for those who go the journey with him/her. Protect him/her from all danger, O God, and comfort him/her in moments of distress. During this time of separation, be for his/her loved ones a source of hope and strength and hasten the day when peace may finally come. Amen. (United Methodist Church)[218]

Presbyterian Church, U.S.A
God, you have delivered us from the scourge of war. May we who have been scarred by war be reconciled to each other, to our enemies, and to you. May we become peacemakers in all that we do. May we always be channels and instruments of your peace. Grant to those who are as yet untouched by war the great gift of continued freedom from the terrible agonies of armed conflict. We ask this in the peace which you alone can provide. Amen.[219]

Lutheran Church, E.L.C.A
Gracious God, your blessings reach to the ends of the earth. We give thanks that you have united us forever through the life, death, and resurrection of Jesus Christ. By the power of

your Holy Spirit, pour out your abundant blessing upon *name/s.* As *he/she/they leave/s* now to serve *his/her/their* country, surround *him/her/them* with your love, keep *him/her/them* from all harm,
and fill *him/her/them* with your Word, that *him/her/them* may walk in your ways, always knowing what is right and good. Comfort all of us with the knowledge that neither death, nor life, nor angels, nor rulers, nor things present, nor things to come, nor powers, nor height, nor depth, nor anything else in all creation, will be able to separate us from the love of God in Christ Jesus our Lord.
Amen [220]

The United Methodist Church has a Shield ceremony for both ends of a deployment to war. The Methodist ceremony included on the previous page is the pre-deployment version but there is also a post-deployment rite. [221] Both ceremonies were created by Navy Chaplain Laura Bender who is endorsed by the United Methodist Church to serve in the Navy. Though originally provided to the Navy and the United Methodist Church, Chaplain Bender's liturgy is also featured in the worship materials for the Presbyterian Church (U.S.A.).[222] The fact that these two major denominations, alongside the Navy, chose to collaborate in the use of this rite makes this ceremony accessible to more American Christians than any other ritual crafted for this purpose in the twenty-first century.

Shield ministry can take other forms besides structured acts of corporate worship. The bed-time prayers of service member's families are an obvious example of the spontaneous nature of this ministry. Most churches in towns that host military bases have a bulletin board or a notice in their newsletter that lists the names of deployed service members who need prayer.[223] National holidays like Memorial Day or Veteran's Day, are occasions for prayers of protection for the armed forces. Military chaplains are frequently called upon to participate in Welcome Home services where prayers of thanksgiving are offered for the unit's safe return. Even churches that are pacifist, and not supportive of the wars waged by this country, have prayer vigils for the troops.[224]

Less conventional practices, at least for some Protestants, are also part of Shield ministry. Many grass-root groups and local congregations have sent objects that are "shields" because of the object's prayer or scripture content. Such an object has been prayed over, or contains a prayer or a verse from Scripture, or some other "shield" to protect deployed warriors who have the object on their person. A very popular item at the start of the Iraq war was the "Shield of Strength."[225] In the original appeal, congregations were encouraged to sponsor the purchase of dog-tag shaped necklaces that had been printed with patriotic symbols and the text from Joshua 1:9 "Be strong and courageous. Do not be frightened, and do not be dismayed, for the LORD your God is with you wherever you go." These "shields" were then shipped to chaplains and other personnel to distribute to the troops. It is still possible to purchase a similar item on the internet.[226] Cloth items like quilts and shawls are sometimes made with the same intent. "The shawl maker begins with prayers and blessings for the recipient, and throughout the process continues in prayer. Upon completion, the shawl is blessed by the group and given to . . . veterans and families of those fallen."[227] While it is impossible to determine the intent of everyone who sent these "shields" or everyone who received them, but the author of *Psalm 91: God's Shield of Protection* attests to her own understanding of this ministry when she says, "to know Psalm 91 can *literally save your life*."[228] The Roman Catholic Church's version of the "Shield of Strength" is the medal of St. Michael. "St. Michael the archangel is the patron saint of soldiers and has provided protection to countless military personnel around the world."[229] The Shield ministry provides ecumenical agreement on the need warriors have for God's protection.

Tambourine Ministry

The U.S. Army has recently discovered a concept that it labels as "resiliency." This concept is applied to troops who have experienced combat and know that other battles are still ahead.[230] The Tambourine ministry could be categorized as a "resiliency" ministry meant to sustain veterans through a long conflict. "Resiliency" is a ". . . soldier's inner strength to face adversity, fear, and hardship during combat with confidence and resolution."[231] In past wars, American warriors used the term "morale" rather than "resiliency." While "morale" is part of "resiliency", "morale" tends to measure the positive aspects of military duty.[232] "Resiliency" on the other hand, acknowledges the darker side of the profession of arms and seeks to find ways for warriors to cope. The original form of "resiliency" for the people of ancient Israel was the Tambourine Ministry.

This ministry was comprised of songs and tambourine dances normalizing the death of enemy combatants. In Exodus 15 the defeat of Pharoah's army is celebrated by Moses and the Israelites. In particular "Miriam the prophetess, the sister of Aaron, took a timbrel in her hand. And all the women went out after her with timbrels and with dances."(Ex 15:20) The judge Deborah ministered to her veterans with a song about how the war was won by a civilian woman driving a spike through the head of the enemy general (Jdg 5:26-27). In a similar instance during the reign of King Saul the women of the cities of Israel brought their tambourines to greet returning veterans with the song "Saul has slain his thousands, and David his ten thousands" (1Sa 18:7). The effect of this ministry was that it sustained David through many campaigns (1Sa 18:16).

The American Civil War engendered many songs still sung even in the twenty-first century like "When Johnny Comes Marching Home Again" and "Dixie."[233] The song from that war's Tambourine Ministry that is still used in churches today is "Battle Hymn of the Republic."[234] "[R]ecently the song was played on Sept. 14, 2001 at both the Washington National Cathedral and St. Paul's Cathedral during memorial services for the victims of the 9/11 attacks."[235] During World War Two some of the secular patriotic songs also included references to God and prayer. One well-known example was "Praise the Lord and Pass the Ammunition."[236] The lyrics describe a chaplain who mans an anti-aircraft gun after the two service members who had been firing the weapon were killed. The title is the song's refrain, put in the mouth of the chaplain who sings, "Praise the Lord and Pass the Ammunition."[237]

Song writers have responded to The Global War on Terror with patriotic lyrics. Songs like "Have You Forgotten"[238] and "Angry American"[239] support a military response to the attack on the World Trade Center and the Pentagon. Both of these songs are secular and it would be a stretch to call them a ministry. A song that is a true contribution to the Tambourine Ministry is Lee Greenwood's "God Bless the USA". The song title is the refrain of a 1984 release for Greenwood. Despite its original purpose of native pride, it has surged in popularity during times of conflict in the U.S, starting with the 1991 Gulf War and most recently with the mission that killed Osama Bin Laden. Churches across America have embraced this song as appropriate for memorial services.[240] The Tambourine ministry is much less common in modern Christianity than in ancient Israel, but "The Battle Hymn of the Republic" and Greenwood's "God Bless the U.S.A." shows that singing still can help veterans to be resilient in the face of a long war.

Compass Ministry

The basis for Compass ministry is seeking God's direction. The key verse is Numbers 27:21 where Eleazer is instructed to inquire (שאל) if the armies of Israel should march or stay in camp. *Strong's Concordance* defines שאל as "to *inquire*; by implication to *request*; by extension to *demand* . . .consult . . .pray . . .wish.."[241] In this study Compass ministry includes any attempt to seek God's direction in a military campaign and does not necessarily mean a formal ritual using a priest. It is clear from the war narratives of Hebrew Scripture that the warriors of Israel understood that success in military operations was dependent on knowing what God was directing them to do.

The first military chaplain recorded in Scripture is Phinehas (Nu 31:6). He serves the detachment of Israelites sent to destroy the Midianites, and his presence upgrades their mission from a raid to a holy war.[242] In the text Phinehas is entrusted with "the holy instruments" (כלי קדש). There is no universal agreement among Biblical scholars about the nature of these objects. One common explanation is that כלי קדש are the Urim and Thummim used by priests for Compass ministry to consult God (Dt 33:8-10).[243] Even if Phinehas did not utilize the Urim and Thummim on the Midianite campaign, he continues to conduct Compass ministry and seek God's direction as shown by the later campaign against the Benjaminites (Jdg 20:18-28). Phinehas' ministry assures the other tribes that Yahweh favors them against their kin, the Benjaminites (Jdg 20:28). Phineas is one of many persons who provide divine direction to the military of ancient Israel.

Sometimes Compass ministry occurs after the battle. Joshua implements Compass ministry after the defeat of his numerically superior forces in the battle for Ai. Joshua consults this vocation to determine which member of the community is responsible for the loss of God's favor. (Jos 7:14). As in the previous narratives the "compass" used to determine God's choice is not specified, but in some manner Joshua is able to ascertain that a certain man sabotaged the war effort by pilfering things devoted to God (Jos 7:1). Once this man and his family are executed the army is able to get back in God's "flow" and the conquest of Ai is accomplished (Jos 8:24). A similar use of the Compass ministry is performed by King Saul. He uses Compass ministry to determine why he did not have God's favor to conduct night operations against the Philistines. Saul wants to know if the person who kindled God's wrath is a member of the royal family or among the people. The Compass ministry informs Saul that the fault lies in his own family and not among his soldiers. (1Sa 14:41) This episode of Compass ministry is unique to military ministry in Scripture because unlike other instances where the person chosen by "compass" is executed, Saul heeds the opinion of his people and does not condemn Jonathan to death.

In addition to these major narratives there are a string of minor episodes recorded in the Hebrew Scriptures that attest to the popularity of Compass ministry among the Israelites. After the death of Joshua the people of Israel conducted a Compass ministry to find out the next commander for their army (Jdg 1:1) Gideon conducts a Compass ministry using the fleece from a sheep before he launches a military campaign against the Midianites and the Amalekites (Jdg 6:36-40). Saul's son Jonathan designs his own Compass ministry based on an enemy sentry's challenge before he leads his armor bearer on a raid of a Philistine outpost (1Sa 14:10). David also conducts Compass services before several of his campaigns (1Sa 23:2; 1Sa 23:4, 1Sa 23:6, 1Sa 23:9-12, 1Sa 30:8; 2Sa 5:19, 2Sa 5:23; 1Ch 14:10;). The fruit of this type of ministry is the confidence David needs to confront the enemy.

As the bellwether of the New Covenant, John the Baptist is also the first person to minister to soldiers in Christian Scriptures. Unlike the prophets or priests of the Hebrew Scriptures interacting with their own veterans, John interacts with military personnel who are in league with Roman authority and are thus outsiders. James Turner Johnson notes, "[T]here was little reason for interaction between serving soldiers and the peaceful townspeople … they inhabited two essentially different worlds."[244] As a consequence ministry to warriors is usually presented like an afterthought rather than intentional inclusion in the service of God. John was actually addressing the children of Abraham when some of the soldiers put their question about post-baptismal conduct to their baptizer. John gives them the benefit of his Compass ministry when says, "Do not forcibly extort anyone, nor accuse *any* falsely. And be content with your wages." (Lk 3:14)

The Acts of the Apostles contains the only intentional ministry to a military person in the New Testament. The centurion Cornelius receives a direct revelation from an angel of God, and asks "What is it, lord?" (Ac 10:4) Thus Peter's ministry is a Compass or "inquiry" ministry as he answers this question for Cornelius. Peter also has an epiphany from this experience and it answers his own inquiry about the vision he has while waiting for Cornelius' emissaries. From this experience Peter is ready when Cornelius' invitation reaches him. (Ac 10:19-20) Peter gives "direction" to Cornelius by preaching the gospel to the centurion and his household. What started out as a "compass" opportunity to a member of the occupying army becomes the starting point for Jews to preach the Good News to Gentiles.

The last time Scripture records the Compass ministry being used to determine whether believers should go to war was in the time of King David (1Ch 14:10). It took over a thousand years from David's campaign for Christianity to institutionalize its own version of the Compass ministry. This institutionalization removed the need for a priest to seek God's intention before warriors go into battle. Christendom now has a set of principles to guide itself about launching a war. These principles are called the Just War Doctrine. The Just War Doctrine ". . . was first compiled, refined, and formalized by Christian theologians and philosophers beginning with Saints Ambrose and Augustine in the fourth and fifth centuries."[245] The main tenets of the Just War doctrine are: (1) War may only be fought to stop an aggressor;

(2) The threat posed by the aggressor must be grave, lasting and certain; (3) All other means to avoid conflict have been exhausted; (4) Success must be likely; (5) The war must not do more damage than the aggressor was going to commit.[246] As Navy Chaplain Neal Moquin informed his marines:

> For centuries, the Just War concept has served as a spiritual guideline for religious communities, a moral compass for our nation's leaders, as well as a source of inspiration for generations of Marines who fought valiantly for our country's freedom, security, and way of life... Making the moral investment before facing combat enables you, as a combatant, the freedom to more fully engage in tactical requirements on the battlefield. Lower stress, reduced anxiety, wholeheartedness in training, a greater sense of impact for the common good, a deeper sense of honor, integrity, and personal worth, greater unit cohesion and spirit, and perhaps a more real sense of the Divine – these are all the potential results of committing morally to the just cause to which you are called.[247]

Military leaders hope that by providing the members of the Armed Services with a moral compass for their participation in war, there will be a lower incidence of Posttraumatic Stress Injury (PTSI) Modern studies show a correlation between moral injuries and PTSI.[248] Whether the Just War doctrine helps reduce PTSI remains to be seen, but it has already replaced the "compass" of ancient Israel.

Tablet ministry

The name for this ministry comes from Exodus 32:15-16 where God gives tablets to Moses containing all the precepts God wants his people to know. After Mount Sinai there are many times in the Hebrew Scripture when the people of Israel perform the Tablet ministry in a civilian setting. The occasion when this service is performed as a veterans' ministry is found in the Book of Joshua.

In the first seven chapters of Joshua the army of Israel conducts a military campaign to conquer the land God has promised. At the destruction of Jericho one of the Israelites does not follow God's instructions (Jos 7:1). This failure to obey God's instructions leads to a humiliating military defeat at the city of Ai (Jos 7:5). The person who disobeyed God is revealed by Compass ministry. This man, and his family, are then executed by the people of Israel (Jos 7:25). The trauma of this event is commemorated by the name the people gave to the location of the execution-The Valley of Grief (Jos 7:26). Eventually the army of Israel follows God's instructions and the city of Ai is destroyed. After the victory the Tablet ministry is performed for the military and their families. Each tribe is assigned a place in the formation around the ark while Joshua reads every word from the tablets of the law to them (Jos 8:33-35). This is the culmination of a series of ministries for veterans conducted at Joshua's behest.

When Joshua instituted this ministry he had just copied the Torah onto tablets of stone (Jos 8:32). Jesus ministered using this ministry after his resurrection. The veterans of the battle in the Garden of Gethsemane were huddled in a safe-house trying to avoid another attack by the Jewish forces (Jn 20:19). Jesus came to them and used the Hebrew Scriptures, and his teachings that are now the Christian canon, to give them an understanding of his death and their continuation of his ministry (Lk 24:44-47). The result of this outreach was that their fear turned to joy (Lk 24:52).

The Tablet Ministry for modern veterans takes many forms. The para-church group Military Ministry includes devotional material as well as Scripture in its Tablet ministry. The fourth of their sixth "pillars" states: "[To] Arm troops in harm's way with spiritual resources. Provide Bibles and devotional materials to chaplains and directly to troops, veterans, and families." The primary way Military Ministries accomplishes this goal is distribution of their "Rapid Deployment Kit" (RDK). "RDK's include a camo-cover New Testament, a 90-day "Our Daily Bread" devotional, and a presentation of the gospel."[249] Over 2.4 million RDKs have been shipped to support warriors with God's word.

There are more Southern Baptist-endorsed chaplains on active duty than any other religion or denomination.[250] The Southern Baptist Convention is also the largest Protestant group among civilians in the United States.[251] The SBC specializes in the Tablet ministry, especially for wounds to the soul. "While it is safe to say that some have strayed from a biblical approach to emotional healing, SBC chaplain training strives to teach emotional health and healing through a Scriptural lens."[252] Two other groups who provide Tablet ministry to members of the military are Officer Christian Fellowship (OCF) and the Navigators. The mission statement of OCF reads "Our Purpose: To glorify God by uniting Christian officers for biblical fellowship and outreach, equipping and encouraging them to minister effectively in the military society."[253] The Navigators has a presence on or near every military base in America. Their description of themselves is "This movement of men and women embraces an unwavering commitment to the Scriptures, a deep reliance on the Holy Spirit, and is fueled by prevailing prayer."[254] Although I have quoted just four of the larger Tablet ministries, countless other organizations like Gideon International and the American Bible Society dedicate considerable resources to provide Bibles and other spiritual resources to members of the military. The Tablet ministry is well resourced and active in American Christianity.

Souvenir Ministry

In modern American English a "souvenir" is an artifact brought back from a journey to a foreign place. In this study a "Souvenir ministry" is a religious practice that has "artifacts" or elements that are foreign to the orthodox practices of Yahweh worship as set forth in Torah. The examples of Souvenir ministry cited in this section are occasions when Hebrew warriors brought back "foreign" religious elements from their campaigns. This ministry is initiated in Joshua 22 when the Eastern tribes show off a souvenir from the Sinai campaign. After their discharge, these veterans (the Reubenites, the Gadites, and the half tribe of Manasseh) build an altar that is a copy of the altar in Shiloh (Jos 22:19). The "souvenir" aspect of their religious practice is that the altar is built without the benefit of the Ark of the Covenant or Levites. (Jos 22:10) The autonomy these Eastern tribes of Israel display is an element of the Sinai campaign (Nu 25:3). The Western tribes dispatch Phinehas to insure the Eastern veterans dispose of this "souvenir" from the Sinai campaign.[255] Only after the Eastern veterans assured the Western tribes that theirs was a memorial altar, not a replacement for the Tabernacle, were the Eastern tribes allowed to continue to reside on the other side of the Jordan river.

Souvenir ministry takes on a more sinister aspect during the time of the Judges. More than any other part of the Hebrew Scriptures, Judges describes a season in history that has the most parallels to the modern Global War on Terror (GWOT). To name one similarity, the Israelites never know where the enemy will strike next. Despite this insecurity, the people in the time of the Judges do not return to the faith of their forefathers as the participants of earlier wars had done (Jdg 2:12). Another similarity with the GWOT is that during the time of the Judges military actions are not conducted against a single adversary, but are a series of campaigns against very different enemies over an extended period of time. The veterans who return from these various campaigns have been exposed to a range of exotic religious practices by various pagan foes (Jdg 2:12).

After the Midianite campaign the Israelites started a Souvenir ministry based on the defining aspect of the Midians. These vanquished Ishmaelites wore ear-rings and their camels wore ornaments, so Gideon sets these souvenirs as the "tribute" veterans usually give to God (Gen 14:20; Jdg 8:24). From the ear-ring and ornament tribute Gideon made an ephod and established a ministry that rivaled the Tabernacle (Jdg 8:27). Thus the heresy that was avoided among the veterans from the Eastern Tribes in Joshua 22 does finally manifest itself among the warriors of Gideon's day.

In a later campaign during the time of the Judges, a warrior named Jephthah plans his post-deployment ministry even before the war is over (Jdg 11:30-31). The Israelites were fighting the Ammonites, a people who worship Milcom/Molech (1Ki 11:5-7). The distinctive characteristic of Milcom/Molech worship was the requirement that parents burn one of their children to death as an offering. God specifically forbids this foreign practice (Lev 18:21). So it is surprising that Jephthah initiated a burned-child ceremony to commemorate his safe return from the war (Jdg 11:31,39). The Hebrew Scriptures say that the offshoot of this Souvenir ministry is still remembered in Israel (Jdg 11:40).

The second chaplain mentioned in Scripture is Jonathan, a Levite who is conscripted for the religious needs of a 600-man detachment from the tribe of Dan. (Jdg 18:16,19) The Danite warriors sought assurance of victory from their chaplain before the battle and Jonathan prophesied victory for their cause. Modern warriors make similar requests to their chaplains.[256] After the victory Jonathan predicted had become a reality, the veterans use an idol from their plunder to establish a Souvenir worship center at Laish, which is in the newly conquered territory. Like Gideon's ephod, the idol at Laish becomes a rival to the Tabernacle in Shiloh (Jdg 18:31). Jonathan and his sons maintain their chaplaincy to this idol until the Assyrians destroy the Northern Kingdom (Jdg 18:30).

After the Israelites transitioned from judges to kings the Souvenir ministry is occasionally manifested by their royalty. King Amaziah marked his victory over the Edomites by transporting their gods back to Judah and conducting foreign rituals to them. (2Ch 25:14) A prophet from Yahweh tried to coax Amaziah to give up these trophies but Amaziah refused. This Souvenir ministry eventually led to Judah's army being defeated and Amaziah being assassinated (2Ch 25:22 & 27). Despite these setbacks a later king resurrected the Souvenir ministry in order to increase his army's military effectiveness. King Ahaz of Judah instituted the worship of the Syrian gods after the Syrian army defeated Judah's army in several battles (2Ch 28:23). Taking the Souvenir ministry to an extreme application King Ahaz eventually locked up the Temple of Yahweh and replaced it with altars to Syrian deities on every street corner (2Ch 28:24).

Christian soldiers frequently have a different praxis of their faith in a war-zone than they do when they are in a peace-time environment.[257] When they bring this practice home, or when the ministry at home offers something other than orthodox Christianity, a Souvenir ministry is present. One type of Souvenir ministry is offered by a reserve Army chaplain at his civilian church. "The Warrior's Journey Home" is a ministry offered by the First Congregational Church in Tallmadge, Ohio. The objective of this group is, "To Listen, To Speak, To Heal."[258] Another branch of this ministry is "Soldier's Heart,"a project that specifically addresses PTSI. This group uses Dr. Edward Tick's book, *War and the Soul*, as its inspiration.[259] Both "The Warrior's Journey Home" and "Soldier's Heart" are non-sectarian.

Although Christian references are not foreign to this ministry, in practice the methods employed are from Native American spiritual traditions and rely on pre-Columbian roots for their power and efficacy.[260] The central symbol is the "talking stick" and the vehicle to apply its power is the veteran's "circle". The mix of Christianity with the aboriginal religions of America makes a very fitting parallel with the way some of the Israelites responded to their returning veterans.

Another Souvenir Ministry for veterans is offered near Fort Carson, Colorado. The He Ska Akicita Inipi (translated as the White Mountain Warriors Lodge) offers a purification ritual for veterans. The rite is performed with a Native American spiritual understanding. The reason it is listed in this study as a Souvenir ministry is because it is recommended by the Army Chaplain's office of Fort Carson. Maj. Cope Mitchell told a reporter "One of the things ... we can learn from part of Native American spirituality is the rites of cleansing, purification after battle . . . The war is nasty; evil is sticky - it sticks to you. This is an option here that has a lot of merit in reaching out that we all need to learn from."[261] With official endorsement like this, both from the Chaplain's Office and the Army website, some Christian warriors are bound to add this "souvenir" to their other war-trophies.

Canteen ministry

Melchizedek is best remembered for the blessing he brought Abraham but he did bring wine and bread also. Not all scholars are convinced that this was a foreshadowing of the Lord's Supper.[262] Professor Bruce McNair notes "Nicolas of Lyra in 1498 reports that some theologians were giving the "perverse explanation" that Melchisedec [sic] brought out bread and wine, not to sacrifice them, but to refresh Abram and his men."[263] If this "perverse explanation" is correct Melchizedek may have been the initiator of the Canteen ministry whose purpose is to provide food to veterans. When Melchizedek brings bread and wine to warriors who had been exposed to deadly peril, he foreshadows the words of a future Hebrew warrior-king who said, "Yea, though I walk through the valley of the shadow of death . . .You prepare a table for me in the presence of my enemies." (Ps 23:4-5) Melchizedek prepared the table for his veterans in the Shaveh valley which is outside Jerusalem. During the period of

Abraham's life, this city was the home of the Jebusites who would become enemies to God's people (2Sa 5:6). Even among Abraham's host there are future enemies. Three Amorites are listed among the warriors in Genesis 14:24. Because Melchizedek has to conduct his vocation with adherents from other religions and even other nations dispersed among the veterans participating in the ritual, he is a fitting example for those who conduct Canteen ministry to the multicultural mix of people who serve in U.S. forces.

Long before David was sitting on the throne of Israel he serves in the Canteen ministry. When his brothers are at the front "Jesse said to his son David, Please take for your brothers an ephah of this parched *grain*, and these ten loaves, and run to the camp to your brothers" (1Sa 17:17). Years later when he himself is in the army, David asks for the Canteen ministry from the priest at Nob saying, "what is under your hand? Give five *loaves* of bread in my hand, or what there is to be found" (1Sa 21:3). Ahimelech the priest gives the bread to David, but this act of ministry alienates King Saul and leads to the destruction of every living thing in the community of Nob (1Sa 22:19). This gives insight into the motivation for communities who refuse to become involved in Canteen ministry.

In the Book of Judges, Gideon asks for food from the villages of Succoth and Penuel. Unlike Nob, these communities refuse to feed his warriors because the outcome of the war has not been decided yet. (Jdg 8:5-8) Succoth and Penuel make a different choice than Ahimelech, but their refusal to become involved in Canteen ministry has severe repercussions too (Jdg 8:16-17). The power of Canteen ministry to influence the outcome of a military campaign is shown in these two narratives. Another indicator of the influence of Canteen ministry is that Jesus cites Ahimelech's ministry to veterans when he is disputing the Pharisees. The point of Jesus' lesson is that the risk the priest took in breaking the law of Moses is more than justified by the mercy he showed to David and his warriors (Mt 12:3-4; Mk 2:25-26).

Feeding the warriors of the Global War on Terror has the participation of corporate sponsorship, not just the Church. From Outback Steakhouse to regional company Rogers Petroleum, corporations have realized that being a canteen for veterans is good for business.[264] Efforts in the church tend to be on a more local level. An individual congregation or sometimes a group of churches in a community gather foodstuffs to mail to warriors. Some churches support units with their Canteen Ministry while other churches choose to support a specific military base. The Fellowship Church of Grapevine, Texas adopted a platoon in Afghanistan and sends their items to that particular unit.[265] First United Church in Plano, Texas supports Bagram Airbase in Afghanistan and allows the chaplains to decide where to distribute their Canteen Ministry. [266] The standard "meal" in the modern Canteen Ministry is the "care package." First United Methodist Church fills their "care packages" with "… snacks and drink mixes, as well as personal hygiene products such as mouthwash, toothpaste and toothbrushes."[267] While the contents may vary according to the organization that sends the care packages, the desire to feed the troops as a work of faith is the same today as when David brought his Canteen Ministry to the army of Israel.

Caisson Ministry

For military funerals at Arlington National Cemetery the U.S. Army uses a caisson to transport the remains of fallen soldiers. "Caisson ministry" is the transportation and/or internment of veterans' remains. The Biblical example that institutes this ministry for ancient Israel's fallen warriors is found in Judges 16:31. In this verse Samson's brothers retrieve Samson's body after it is crushed under the remains of the Philistine temple. Samson's family makes the trip to Gaza to transport the body back to the family tomb located between Zorah and Eshtaol. The next instance of Caisson ministry is in 1 Samuel 31 where the men of Jabesh-Gilead risk life and limb to recover the body of Saul and his son Jonathan from enemy control and return them to friendly soil (1Sa 31:13). King David complete the Caisson ministry initiated by the men of Jabesh-Gilead and interred Saul and Jonathan's remains in their family tomb (2Sa 21:12-14).

When modern American warriors fall in battle their remains are transported back to the U.S. by the government so a Caisson Ministry in the footsteps of the people of Jabesh-Gilead is not really possible. Instead the modern form of this ministry deals with internment ceremonies and honoring the graves of fallen warriors. Since the government transports the bodies of the deceased, the first phase of ministry for those killed in war is often performed by military chaplains who conduct memorial services for the fallen warrior before the body leaves the theater of war. If the warrior's family wishes, a military funeral at the time of internment of remains can also be arranged.[268]

Not all Caisson Ministry is performed for those who die in battle. Many veterans who survive their war request a military presence to be included in their funeral as well as the religious component. Since the largest part of the United States does not have a military chaplain near enough to support funeral honors for the majority of veterans' internments, organizations like the Veterans of Foreign Wars and the American Legion have chaplains to provide the Caisson Ministry to their members. These chaplains are drawn from the ranks of the veterans' organizations' members.[269] The Caisson Ministry provided by their chaplains has grown in importance as the age of their membership has increased.[270]

The chaplains of veterans' organizations also conduct Memorial Day services. Memorial Day is a public holiday that came into being after the Civil War and is meant to honor those who died for their country. Many churches include some aspect of the holiday in their Sunday service.[271] Decorating of graves with flags and other signs of respect are the trademarks of this holiday. Since it is a national holiday, many other organizations partake in this Caisson Ministry. Perhaps the group that has a connection with the fallen nearly as poignant as the men of Jabesh-Gilead is Gold Star Moms. In order to be a member of this group a mother must have lost one of her children in war. Every year this organization's program of "Wreath's Across America" decorates thousands of graves of fallen warriors.[272]

Exit Ministry

This ministry is initiated by a man named Shimei who tells King David and his army to צא (2Sa 16:7). *Strong's Concordance* defines צא as "to *go* (causatively *bring*) *out* . . . come out . . .depart . . .escape . . . get away. .."[273] Shimei not only curses David but throws rocks at him and his staff as the army parades through the town. Shimei condemns David and his military on moral and political grounds with the words,

"Go out, O man of blood, O man of Belial. Jehovah has returned on you all the blood of the house of Saul, in whose place you have reigned" (2Sa 16:7-8). The key aspect of the Exit ministry is disapproval of the military, its leaders, its members or an action undertaken by any of the preceding parties. In this first Biblical encounter with the Exit ministry the warriors are exhausted and need refreshment when they camp for the night (2Sa 16:14).

Another application of the Exit ministry is found in David's attitude towards his own troops after the death of Absalom (2Sa 19:1-3). The king chose to focus on the blood that was shed and to ignore the actual strategic victory gained by his troops. General Joab summarized the mindset of David when he says, "You have made it clear that your officers and men mean nothing to you. I can see that you would be quite happy if Absalom were alive today and all of us were dead. " (2Sa 19:6) As a result these warriors have to use their own resources to reintegrate into their community since the cultural leader disapproved of their work. A similar fate awaits the now leaderless army of Absalom which has no one to legitimize their sacrifice. These veterans also have to make their own re-integration happen (2Sa 19:8).

In the original Exit ministry Shimei rejects the warriors, their politics and their military actions. A Christian group is considered an Exit ministry in this study if the organization views any aspect of military action to be against God's precepts. Some organizations included in this category oppose only a particular war. Other organizations reject any violence including self-defense. Exit ministry includes groups that support warriors and their profession but treat their spiritual injuries as if the wounds are the result of sin. It also incorporates denominations that are pacifist in political persuasion but still minister to warriors through prayer and hospitality. All these options are considered to be in the category of Exit ministry.

There are "Peace churches" that claim descent from the pacifism of the early church. Mennonites, Church of the Brethren, and Quakers are examples of "peace churches" that have a tradition of pacifism.[274] The rejection of bloodshed has not prevented some of the members of Peace churches from serving in the military as non-combatants.[275] Additionally, some mainline denominations have peace societies within their polity that serve as the anti-war voice for their denomination. One such society in the Episcopalian Church is the Episcopalian Peace Fellowship (EPF). The rejection of war has not meant a rejection of the warrior. Bill Graham, a member of EPF for 50 years, believes "that churches need to include military concerns in worship prayers, rituals, and songs. This worship proclamation means even more when paired with practical support for armed forces members and their families."[276] Graham's church, St. Mary's Holly-Rushville (Episcopal) Church in Nebraska conducts their Exit ministry from this perspective.

An article by the United Methodist News Service began its story about a group of military chaplains with the words, "In the name of Jesus Christ you are forgiven."[277] This is because the official position of the denomination towards war is "We believe war is incompatible with the teachings and example of Christ."[278] This interpretation is also echoed in the *Catechism of the Catholic Church*, "The fifth commandment forbids the intentional destruction of human life. Because of the evils and injustices that accompany all war, the Church insistently urges everyone to prayer and to action so that the divine Goodness may free us from the ancient bondage of war."[279] The Pontifical Council for Justice and Peace pronounced every war as "unnecessary massacre" and "never an appropriate way to resolve problems that arise between nations."[280] Both of these denominations endorse chaplains to serve the military but the official policy of the United Methodist Church and the Roman Catholic Church is an Exit ministry that echoes Shimei's claim that service members who participate in a war are sinners in need of reconciliation with God, church and community.

In order to assist war veterans in this reconciliation, the Methodist and Catholic Churches offer different forms of Exit rites. The response of the Roman Catholic Church to the violation of the fifth commandment is not veteran-specific but is required of any sinner. In order for a person to be "reconciled" to God and the church for participation in "unnecessary massacre", the sacrament of Reconciliation is the portal. In this ritual the veteran as "sinner" expresses his or her sorrow and the priest grants absolution. The June 2012 Missal for the American branch of the Catholic Church described the effect of this rite "The church teaches that when we perform these outward signs, our sins are washed away, and we are made right with God once more."[281]

The Methodist rite for Exit ministry takes a community approach. The liturgy for "An Order for Welcoming Service Members Returning from War" has already been mentioned in the section discussing Shield ministry. This particular ceremony has elements to discharge several aspects of post-deployment experience for the congregation and the veteran. Though not labeled as an "Exit ministry," the condemnation is implied in the pastoral invitation to silent prayer ". . .you may have been required to act in ways that are outside the parameters of civilized behavior. . . I ask you now, in the presence of this community of faith, to offer up a silent prayer for all that . . . grieves your spirit and weighs heavily on your heart."[282] In American culture the Miranda Warning may allow for silence not to be construed as guilt, but in the Bible silence is the same as agreement (Ps 50:21). The Presbyterians add their own Exit ministry commentary to the Methodist rite:

> We have found that many returning veterans are haunted by guilt over the terrible things they have either committed or witnessed. Formulas of confession need to be worded in a way that allows veterans to transfer moral weight of the event(s) that violated their conscience from themselves to the community that is authorized to declare the word of forgiveness in the name of the Lord. Public confession restores persons to God, to themselves, and to their communities."[283]

The Roman Catholic Church, the United Methodist Church, the Presbyterian Church U.S.A. and a host of other denominations participate in the World Council of Churches.[284] This organization initiated a ten year campaign called "The Decade to Overcome Violence" which had as one of its goals the exclusion of any positive teaching based on war. Like the Methodists, the World Council of Churches believes war is a betrayal of the gospel. [285] The Decade initiative is just one sample of a trend in parts of Christianity reflecting a disdain of all things connected with war. [286] Depending on how far a particular organization's Exit ministry excludes any positive impression of military service will effect whether the veterans of said organization have to imitate King David's men and make their own way back into society (2 Sa 19:3).

In the context of ministry to modern veterans there exists in America's protestant Christianity a link between Exit ministry and the Bandage ministry of healing. In 2 Samuel 16:8 Shimei charged David with "mischief" (רעה), and some of today's ministries for PTSI are built around the warrior confessing their "mischief." *Strong's Concordance* translates רעה as "*bad ,. . . evil* (naturally or morally). . . affliction, calamity, . . . harm,. . . mischief." [287] One of the first steps to healing in Military Ministries' *The Combat Trauma Healing Manual* called "spiritual breathing." The goal is "Out with the bad, in with the good."[288] The "exhale" cycle is confessing personal sins. It should be noted that confessing personal sins was covered in the *Healing Manual* two pages previously and is brought up again two pages after the spiritual breathing exercise as part of the instructions to reading the Bible (37,39,41). The *Manual* returns to confessing sin in the sixth chapter that is entitled, "How Do I Move On?" It is an entire chapter on guilt and repentance (79-87). It includes a "Memorial Project." This rite is centered on a list of the warrior's sins and God's forgiveness of them. This rite does not conclude the need to confess guilt as part of the treatment of PTSI. In the eighth chapter that purports to rebuild the warrior, the initial building block is "Closing Doorways." The metaphor is an allusion to Genesis 4:7 where "sin crouches at the door." One of the suggested sins crouching at the door of the veteran's heart is ". . . an insatiable urge to kill developing after the firefight" which started after being "traumatized in a firefight"(114). This expectation of senseless violence from a veteran is in keeping with Shimei's accusation, "Go out, O man of blood" (2Sa 16:7). These highlights along with the numerous other references to guilt in *The Combat Trauma Healing Manual* make it clear that this is an Exit ministry too.

The expectation of "mischief" in veterans is also present in *Welcome Them Home Help Them Heal,* the book that supports the Bandage Ministry of the Elim Lutheran Church of Blackhoof, Minnesota. The authors state that "any intentional perpetration of harm towards human beings, their livelihood and their belongings can cause grave moral injury and damage the relationship to one's self, others and God."[289] This book makes clear that even witnessing these events can wound a warrior's conscience.[290] The book asks churches to be prepared to set up rites of Reconciliation, the Exit ministry mentioned previously in the Catholic Church.[291] Also suggested for individual warrior's homes are Heart-Cleansing Rituals" where the veteran can hear his or her family members share how they were hurt by the deployment.[292] The veteran is encouraged to "interact" which with what family members have shared and closes this part of the ritual with a "confessional" prayer.

Bandage Ministry

The Bandage Ministry is a restoration ministry. The title for this ministry is derived from the Hebrew word אסף which means, "restore . . .put all together, receive, recover . . ."[293] In 2 Kings 5:3 a Hebrew captive tells the wife of an Assyrian general that a prophet in Israel can אסף her husband of his leprosy. Na'aman, the Assyrian general, acts on this information and seeks out the Bandage ministry of the prophet Elisha. Even though Na'aman is an Assyrian warrior who formerly has worshipped the national gods of Syria, the healing he receives from Elisha converts him into a Yahweh worshipper (2Ki 5:15). Na'aman is not the only enemy soldier to receive the Bandage ministry from Elisha. In 2 Kings 6 Syrian raiders attack Israel and are blinded by Yahweh (2Ki 6:18). In their sightless state Elisha leads them into captivity in Samaria. After the enemy soldiers are enclosed within the walls Elisha prays and restores their sight. Not only is their sight restored but Elisha adds hospitality to this Bandage ministry and as a result the raiders stop coming into Israel (2Ki 6:23).

In a parallel to Elisha, the first occasion that Jesus ministers to a member of the military, he is asked to conduct an act of Bandage ministry for an officer from an opposing army. (Mt 8:5-6; Lk 7:2-3) The significant aspect of this encounter for the current study is the way in which Jesus meets the need of the Roman official. In his request to Jesus, the centurion asks that Jesus operate the Bandage ministry according to military protocol, ". . .but say a word, and my servant will be healed. For I also am a man set under authority, having under me soldiers. And I say to one, Go, and he goes; and to another, Come, and he comes; and to my servant, Do this, and he does *it*" (Lk 7:7-8). Jesus favors the centurion and not only heals the servant, but performs the action through the spoken word just like a commanding officer in the military. Jesus uses this example to encourage the rest of Israel to have faith in him. (Lk 7:9) This was not the only occasion Jesus implements the Bandage ministry to a warrior from an opposing force. During the fight in the Garden of Gethsemane, Jesus heals the amputated ear of Malchus, one of the soldiers from the high priest. (Lk 22:51) In this act of restoration Jesus lives out a lesson also recorded in Luke, "[L]ove your enemies, and do good . . .hoping for nothing *in return*." (Lk 6:35) As all four Gospels record, this Bandage ministry is followed by the minister's crucifixion.

The sheer number of warriors who have returned from war with physical and/or spiritual issues has elicited many churches and para-church organizations to establish Bandage ministries. The healing and restoration of a Bandage ministry can take many varieties of form because "No two veterans have the same war experience, nor, upon returning from war do they face exactly the same reintegration challenges. Likewise, veterans heal and recover in their own ways and along their own timelines."[294] Differences in the theology of groups providing Bandage ministry to warriors adds a further level of diversification.

Some of the Bandage ministries use liturgy to heal veterans. The First Presbyterian Church of Birmingham, Michigan offers an annual Veteran's Processional as a healing service. Prior to the service, the worship planners contact veterans from different wars and invite them to participate. The service begins with these warriors carrying in "the Bible, the baptismal pitcher, the communion cup and plate. .. It seemed that the memories of all who had served merged with the promise of hope as these men walked together in footsteps of faith."[295] First Presbyterian's perspective on healing through liturgy was influenced by a branch of the Lutheran church. [296] The Lutheran church mentioned on the Presbyterian webpage is the Elim Lutheran Church of Blackhoof in Barnum, Minnesota and their book for Bandage ministry, *Welcome Them Home Help Them Heal*. [297]

Despite the rural location of this church, its manual has received national attention and is being distributed by the chaplains of the Veterans Administration.[298] The sixth chapter of the book contains twelve spiritual exercises (rituals) for churches to offer during the calendar year for the healing of veterans. These ceremonies ". . . create a climate of healing and communicate a strong sense of solidarity with all those recovering from the wounds of war."[299]

A good example of non-liturgical approach to healing is Military Ministry. This organization is a branch of Campus Crusade for Christ and is one of the five largest para-church organizations that address the needs of veterans.[300] Like the Elim church in Minnesota, Military Ministry also centers their Bandage ministry around a book. For Military Ministry that book is *The Combat Trauma Healing Manual: Christ-centered Solutions for Combat Trauma* written by Christopher Adsit.[301] Campus Crusade was founded by Bill Bright who advocated *The 4 Spiritual Laws*.[302] That same ethos is present in Military Ministry's approach to healing in *The Combat Trauma Healing Manual.* The instructions for "Constructing Your Healing Environment" includes this guidance ". . . you need to *know* the laws, and you need to *obey* the laws."[303] The "laws" referred to are not magical steps but a synthesis of Biblical principles for healing as set forth by Rev. Adsit. Prayer, reading Scripture, and participating in a community of faith are just a few of these healing steps suggested to the warrior and/or family member to heal the effects of war. A similar prescription is found on the website for the internet Bandage ministry of "Combat Faith". Founded by Viet Nam veteran Allen Clark, Combat Faith advocates, "[T]he global remedy for PTSD. . . comes through the following of the faith disciplines of prayer, reading of Scripture and corporate involvement in a faith community, the church."[304] This .summary of the restorative process is the core for many Protestant Bandage ministries seeking to heal the soul- wounds received from war.

Wash Ministry

Sometimes a war narrative can contain more than one type of military ministry. Such is the case with Numbers 31. This narrative has already been discussed as an example of the Compass ministry as the Israelites marched to war with Phinehas as their chaplain. However, when the warriors return, Phinehas' ministry is subsumed under civilian control. Moses and Eliezer direct the veterans' re-integration (Nu 31:12-13 and 21). What occurs under civilian leadership is a Wash ministry. The name for this ministry is based on the Hebrew word חטא. In Numbers 31:20 Moses commands the Israelites to חטא themselves, all their clothing, and anything else that cannot withstand fire. *Strong's Concordance* defines חטא as, "A primitive root; properly to *miss*; . . . by inference to *forfeit. . .expiate, repent,* . . . cleanse, . . . purge, purify. .."[305] As the definition in *Strong's Concordance* indicates, this is a complicated word that contains many nuances. For the purposes of this study, this complex action has been synthesized into the single word "wash" which is used to signify the act of cleansing.

Moses and Eliezer did not want death-shadow to contaminate the main Israelite camp so they quarantined the veterans and their war-booty (including female captives) until everyone who with death-exposure had been washed (Nu 31:19). The method and schedule of this post-war wash is described in Numbers 19. Scholar David P. Wright has studied these two passages and concludes, "[S]imilarities in language and prescription show that Num. xxxi 19ff. presupposes and is dependent upon the legislation concerning purification from corpse-contamination found in ch. xix."[306] The text of Numbers 19 says everything in a place containing a dead body, whether it touches the corpse or not, is contaminated and must be ritually decontaminated before it can be returned to the community and religious involvement.

At Numbers 31:19-20, Moses treats his returning army, enemy P.O.W.'s, and even the spoils of war as if they had come from a place of death. All participants in the Midianite campaign had to be cleansed in a religious ritual before they can have a normal life again. The substance prescribed to "wash" the veterans is the ash-slurry from the red heifer described in Numbers 19. Scholar Joseph Blau notes, "Another unique aspect linking these two passages is a liquid called "water of separation" (מים נדה). Among all the treatises on funeral practices and the handling of remains in the Hebrew Scripture, only these passages utilize this substance."[307] Although the rite outlined in Numbers 19 appears designed for individuals and families who have access to the Tabernacle (Nu 19:4), the narrative in Numbers 31 indicates that the ashes of a heifer can be applied in a rustic setting away from established venues for sacred activities. In addition to the heifer-ash "wash" from chapter 19, the veterans in chapter 31 are commanded to give a portion of the booty to God and to the civilian population. (Nu 31:26-30) The formula used for this redistribution of war-booty is more sophisticated than the one used by Abraham in Gen 14, but this similarity between Moses' ministry and Melchizedek's ministry is worth noting (Gen 14:20).

The rite described in Numbers 19 and Numbers 31 is the only death-shadow purification ritual in the Hebrew Scriptures and there is no mention in the Gospels of Jesus empowering the disciples to conduct cleansing from death-shadow. While he walked the earth, Jesus was the only "wash" for death-shadow purification. A previous section of this study has already focused on Matthew's declaration that Jesus is the fulfillment of Isaiah's prophecy that people in Northern Israel suffering from death-shadow would be delivered (Isa 9:2; Mt 4:14-16).

In essence, delivering someone from death-shadow is the goal of the Wash Ministry. The Gospel of Mark contains a narrative that describes one such deliverance. A man, who may have been a veteran,[308] approaches Jesus. This man (called Decapolitan in this study) has been psychogenically injured by exposure to a death-filled environment. He is no longer able to function according to the rules of society and he thinks God is his enemy (Mk 5:3,7). After Jesus commands the "uncleanness" out of Decapolitan, his psychogenic stability returns, and he is able to commune with both humans and God (Mk 5:15). It is an ironic detail of this narrative that the unclean spirits who call themselves by military nomenclature end up in creatures which commit suicide rather than live under the influence of death-shadow. Jonathan Shay notes that for many Vietnam veterans, suicide seemed like the only form of purification available.[309]

The author of Hebrews states that the ability to wash people of their death-shadow has now been given to the Church. The Church is able to do this because Jesus is now their high priest in the heavenly sanctuary (Hebrews chapters 5 through 10). It is clear from the author's thesis on Jesus' heavenly ministry that the new cleansing solution for death-shadow only became operative after Jesus' death. This Final Covenant ministry is patterned after the elements in

Numbers 19. In Hebrews 9:13-14 the Church is told "For if . . . the ashes of a heifer sprinkling the unclean sanctifies to the purifying of the flesh, how much more shall the blood of Christ . . . purge your conscience from dead works to serve *the* living God?" The author of Hebrews points the way for Christians to understand the transition of "wash" ministry under the First Covenant to the wash ministry the Church is supposed to provide. Under the First Covenant the heifer-ash slurry was applied to a person's body to purify him or her from death-shadow. Now in the Final Covenant, the blood of Jesus is can be "applied" to the conscience of someone who is tainted by death-shadow.

Hebrews 9:14 uses the words νεκρών 'εργων rather than "death-shadow" to describe the contaminating agent of the conscience. This phrase is commonly translated as "dead works". A literal translation is "works of corpses"[310] and a similar definition by author Gary Selby is "works of death."[311] Either way these two Greek words are translated, there is a congruency with death-pollution and heifer ashes in the First Covenant and a death-shadowed conscience and the blood of Jesus in the Final Covenant: The person who is exposed to death is not able to access their faith and has to be purified of their exposure to death before returning to worship and the community.[312]

The author of Hebrews believes that in the Final Covenant it is the person's συνείδησις (conscience) that needs to be "washed" in order to restore communion with God. *Thayer's* defines συνείδησις as "the consciousness of anything . . .the soul . . . prompting to do the former [good] and shun the latter [bad], commending one, condemning the other."[313] *Strong's* defines συνείδησις as "a prolonged form of συνείδω" which is further defined as "to *understand* or *become aware*, and to *be conscious [of]*".[314] Originally in Greek literature συνείδησις was a morally neutral term that focused on a person's inner awareness of themselves.[315] This word (συνείδησις) is found five times in Hebrews.[316] Four of these occurrences feature prominently in the book's assertion that Jesus has opened our access to God. In Hebrews συνείδησις is a person's internal awareness of what he or she has experienced that would allow or hinder access to God. According to Selby, the author of Hebrews believes the συνείδησις has the ability to be effected by, or to remember participating in, "works of death" (νεκρῶν ἔργων, 9:14).[317] Psychological studies have shown that, "One of the most pervasive effects of traumatic exposure is the challenge that people experience to their existential beliefs concerning the meaning and purpose of life, particularly at risk is the strength of their religious faith and the comfort that they derive from it."[318] The promise of Hebrews 9:13-14 is that through Wash ministry, "Jesus' sacrifice cleanses the conscience, [and] it allows for *unhindered access to God*."[319]

Despite this Scriptural commission, no such ministry or rite exists to purify the consciences of veterans injured by death-shadow. The lack of such ministry has been noticed by even secular sources. VA psychologist Jonathan Shay has made a public plea for a purification ritual to purge returning warriors of the unhealthy psychological aspects of combat.[320] Shay's opinion is echoed by David Bosworth, a theologian who has examined the subject of war-pollution. Bosworth states "[S]ince American veterans live in a society that has no explicit system of purity, they have no access to purification."[321] He suggests that the ritual described in the narrative of Numbers 31 ". . . may provide a useful resource for transitioning soldiers from combat to home life."[322]

CHAPTER 6

New Wash Ministry

The American Psychiatric Association has set the third diagnostic criterion for Posttraumatic Stress Injury as "avoidance."[323] Perhaps that is why the Veterans Administration and the psychological community have been able to document that direct confrontation is the most effective therapy for PTSI.[324] As recorded above, author Robin Green believes "liturgy" establishes a milieu where "direct confrontation" is possible. This suggests that liturgy, employing God's instrument for death-purification, will be the most effective response for the Church to use in ministry to veterans with PTSI.

Merriam-Webster's Dictionary defines "liturgy" as, "a rite or a body of rites prescribed for public worship."[325] In this study rite, ritual, and liturgy will be used without distinction as meaning the same thing: "[A] patterned activity with symbolic meaning."[326] According to pastor and research professor Herbert Anderson, "ritual" is for moving from one state of being to another.[327] In the case of a purification ritual, the transition is from a state of contamination to a state of aboriginal composition. The purification ritual proposed by this study receives the veteran polluted by "death-shadow" and restores him or her to the state of grace he or she enjoyed prior to exposure to war. Since "death-shadow" is used in this study as a synonym for PTSI, and PTSI has both a physical and a psychological component, the proposed purification ritual will also be a healing ritual. Anderson describes "healing" as, ". . . a process of restoring bodily well-being, emotional wholeness, mental-functioning, and/or spiritual vitality."[328] In a sense, a veteran is "healed" by being "purified."

Two Rites from Other Religions

Many cultures already possess and employ purity rituals for veterans. The best documented warrior-cleansing rituals in recent history were conducted in Mozambique following the conclusion of their civil war in 1992. The goal of these rituals was not "regression" to pre-war innocence. "He does not become the person he was before (and that would be impossible, since he most often left home as a child or a youngster, and he is now a man), but he became a "person like the others."[329] Key concepts that guide these purification rites are: 1) the veteran poses a spiritual threat to himself and his community; 2) the living can be spiritually-infected by exposure to death; 3) physical illness or symptoms are manifestations of the veteran's spiritual health; 4) non-combatants who witnessed military actions also must undergo decontamination; 5) the ceremonies follow a *rites de passage* structure with no verbalization of the reasons for expurgation.[330] The ceremonies were conducted according to a belief in "local spirits" of the tribes of Mozambique and healers from the veteran's community presided at these rites.[331] Through these cleansing rituals the Mozambican people were able not only to receive back their own veterans into the community, but also enemy veterans who fought against them.[332]

Native American culture has a tradition of warrior-purification rituals and some of these rituals are beginning to surface around U.S. military bases. The White Mountain Warrior's Lodge (*He Ska Akicita Inipi* in the Lakota language) at Fort Carson, Colorado offers a sweat lodge ceremony ". . . to pray and purify as a way of transitioning from warrior to non-combatant."[333] The format of an *inipi* ceremony is derived from the teachings of the tribal elders and adapted by the experiences of the person leading the ceremony.[334] The actual sweat lodge is constructed to be a holy space, usually in the form of a tent, or other portable structure. The Lakota tribe was traditionally nomadic and this is reflected in the architecture of their tent "sanctuary." As the polar opposite of the "death-house" of Numbers 19:14, the sweat lodge has the power to re-establish the sacred.[335] Like the cleansing rituals of other cultures, the sweat lodge, ". . . help[s] returning warriors come back into the circle of relatives, friends, clan, and community."[336] This purification rite is not only a spiritual cleansing but also eliminates physical pollution as well.[337] While originally practiced by Native American men, the sweat lodge purification ceremony of the White Mountain Warrior's Lodge is open to men and women of any nation, with pride of place going to newly returned veterans.[338]

These two examples of cleansing ceremonies were included to demonstrate that culture provides the structure within which purification can occur. The Mozambicans use methods that are indigenous to their tribal practices. The Lakota ritual is conducted using the resources and traditions of the nomads of the American Plains. A similar standard is required for the introduction of a purification rite in the Church. Professor Elaine Ramshaw notes, "For the images that shape Christian ritual, that language must be theological, biblical, catholic, and confessional."[339] The Evangelical United Brethren Church stated this requirement using stronger language, "Whatever is not revealed in or established by the Holy Scriptures is not to be made an article of faith . .."[340] The decontamination rite for PTSI/death-shadow proposed by this study will follow these dictates. Yet this ritual is also for a particular sub-section of Christian people- those who have returned from war. Therefore this ritual is also shaped by the culture of the U.S. military.

The Components

The ancient Hebrew warrior purification ritual, called in this study the Wash Ministry, is set forth in Numbers 19 and executed in Numbers 31. The core components of the ritual are: a special liquid (Nu 19:17; Nu 31:23); a place of quarantine (Nu 19:9; Nu 31:19); a schedule of lustrations (Nu 19:12; Nu 31:19); and the method of lustration (Nu 19:18; Nu 31:23).

The special liquid was made from the ashes of a red heifer (Nu 19:9). When these ashes were mixed with water it created the "waters of separation"(מים נדה). This slurry has been the subject of extensive study. Joseph Blau of Columbia University remarks, "In the Mishnah and also in the Tosefta, an entire tractate, called Parah, of the order Taharoth, is devoted to minute examination of the traditional regulations for the preparation of the water of purification from the ashes of the red Heifer."[341] Jewish scholars speculate that the heifer ash-water solution was constituted only nine times.[342] If the ashes of a red heifer were still required in a Christian purification ritual for death-shadow there would be no way to re-institute this rite. Blau notes that since the destruction of the Second temple, ". . . and the consequent end to all priestly rituals, there would have been no further opportunity to prepare the ashes or the mixture."[343] Blau is speaking about the ability of the Levitical priesthood to produce the "waters of separation." Christian Scriptures teach that the Temple and, more significantly, the Levitical priesthood have been superseded by the priesthood of Jesus.

Starting in Chapter five, and continuing through chapters six and seven, the Epistle to the Hebrews explains how Jesus fulfills the ministry of Melchizedek, the primordial member of a pre-Levitical order of priests. Melchizedek is the earliest priest mentioned in the Hebrew Scriptures (Ge 14:18). He greets Abraham after the first war recorded in Scripture, and blesses Abraham, who responds by giving a tithe to this priest (Ge 14:19-20). This act of receiving Abraham's sacrifice is used by the author of Hebrews to prove the superiority of the Melchizedek's priesthood over the Levitical priesthood that was established many generations after this ceremony (Heb 7:5-9). A significant part of Jesus' authority, according to the Epistle to the Hebrews, rests on Melchizedek's ordination and office which is declared in the Psalms, "Jehovah has sworn, and will not repent, You are a priest forever after the order of Melchizedek" (Ps 110:4).

Seven times the epistle to the Hebrews confirms that Jesus continues in this ministry. [344] Verse 7:1 of the epistle sets Melchizedek's ministry in Genesis within the context of a ritual for returning warriors: "For this Melchizedek, king of Salem and priest of the Most High God, met Abraham returning from the slaughter of the kings and blessed him." The warrior-transitioning-to-citizen aspect of the order of Melchizedek is established beyond question in the next verse (Heb 7:2) when the author explains that Melchizedek as the king of Salem was also "king of peace" (βασιλεὺς εἰρήνη). Thus the "king of peace" blesses the one "returning from the slaughter."

The destruction of the Second Temple made it impossible for the sons of Levi to continue their priestly duties, but this event had no effect on Jesus who is a priest at the "greater and more perfect tabernacle, not made with hands" (Heb 9:11). His access to this indestructible sanctuary means that Jesus can continue the death-shadow "special liquid" ministry. The text of Hebrews 9:13-14 asks, "For if the blood of bulls and of goats and the ashes of a heifer sprinkling the unclean sanctifies to the purifying of the flesh, how much more shall the blood of Christ . . . purge your conscience from dead works to serve *the* living God?" Through the use of terms that are distinct to Numbers 19, this epistle establishes the fact that the "blood of Christ" has become the new "waters of separation."

If this is so, the question must be asked whether Christians can access this "special liquid" for terrestrial rituals? The answer lies in the last ceremony Jesus instituted before his crucifixion. At the Last Supper Jesus told his disciples that the cup he blessed that night contained his blood (Mt 26:26-27; Mk 14:23-24; Lk 22:20). This ceremony, and its significance, is reiterated in the first epistle to the church in Corinth, ""This cup is the New Covenant in My blood" (1Co 11:25). A more significant statement concerning the communion cup as the access point for Jesus' blood is the assertion in 1 Corinthians 10:16, "The cup of blessing which we bless, is it not the communion of the blood of Christ?" The Greek word for "communion" (κοινωνία) in this text is defined by *Strong's Concordance* as "participation" and also "distribution."[345] Whether one chooses to use "participation" or "distribution", this verse still connects the cup of blessing with the blood of Jesus. This study suggests that through the rite of the Last Supper Christians have access to the new "waters of separation" and can thus implement the death-shadow decontamination ritual for veterans polluted by war.

The Structure

In the rite of Communion, the Church re-enacts Jesus' final meal with his disciples. The structure of the ceremony is driven by the events recorded in Scripture. This study proposes a similar approach to the structure of a warrior cleansing rite. The process prescribed by God in Numbers thirty-one is the event the Church can re-enact to institute a death-shadow cleansing experience. The general outline of the process will be decided by the interaction between the particular contaminants of war and the remedy inspired by God's word.

In the military version of the death-shadow ritual, Moses and Eleazar the High Priest took the general instructions for decontamination in Numbers chapter 19 and applied them to returning veterans in Numbers 31.[346] In both chapter 19 and the later application by Moses on the plains of Moab, the cleansing took place over a seven day period (Nu 19:16; Nu 31:19). In order to keep the connection between the ancient rite and the one proposed for current veterans, this chronology should be re-presented, though it need not be done literally.[347] Anthropologist Roy Rappaport notes that re-presenting time is a common feature of rituals, "All societies . . .are faced with the task of constructing time, not simply for the coordination of social life but to provide roads for each individual's temporal experience to follow."[348] One way to demarcate the "days" in the new rite is to set a particular "mission" for each period. In military vernacular a "mission" is a task set by a command element.[349] Much like the seven days of Creation (Ge 1-2:1) are delineated by the tasks that God accomplished, the seven "days" of this warrior quarantine should have particular "missions" that are undertaken. These "missions" could take the form of a lesson, a small group activity, or some other therapeutic or cathartic gesture that connects the veteran's experience to God using the Scriptural narrative.

The first "mission" (thus "day") is to establish the garrison. Moses personally met the veterans before they could reintegrate and commanded them to form this garrison (Nu 31:13 &19). The guiding principle for this task is "separation", an element present in most rituals that change a person's status.[350] In the Hebrew Scriptures any ritual involving returning veterans happened away from the normal community. Besides the narrative under discussion some notable examples are: Melchizedek met Abram while he was still in the Shaveh valley (Ge 14:17); The army of the departing Eastern tribes consecrated an altar on the border between their land and Israel (Jos 22:10); Samuel built a sacred pillar between Mizpah and Shen at the conclusion of the Philistine invasion (1Sa 7:12-17); After his victory over the Ammonites and Moabites, King Jehoshaphat had a worship service in the Beracah valley before returning to Jerusalem (2Ch 20:26). For the modern cleansing rite, this separation could be symbolized by conducting the ceremony at a time other than the regularly scheduled congregational worship services. Likewise, since Moses' veterans did not have access to the Tabernacle during their quarantine, the modern host church's sanctuary should not be the first place the veterans gather.

In the Scriptural narrative, the returning veterans are met by Moses and Eleazar, who are veterans themselves of earlier campaigns. From a sociologist's point of view these two veterans of past wars represent "ritual elders", a common method of establishing sacred time and space.[351] In a modern rite the newest crop of returning veterans should be welcomed into the "garrison" by veterans of earlier deployments. The reception of one "generation" by its ancestors is a non-verbal expression of continuity, a key ingredient in an effective ritual.[352] Just as Moses and Eleazar were the ones who directed the establishment of the Israelite garrison, the "ritual elders" of modern veterans can facilitate the initial arrival and processing of returning warriors to this cleansing rite. .

The second "day" could be conducting a "census" or "roll-call". Moses had his leaders conduct a roll-call in the garrison outside the main Israelite camp (Nu 31:49). The process of mustering the troops for accountability is done in all branches of the U.S. military but it was also a regular part of the military operations of ancient Israel (1Sa 14:17). The purpose of the "roll-call" in this cleansing rite is to allow the participating veterans to honor the fallen members of their unit and to symbolically restore the unit to its pre-deployment structure. Failure to acknowledge the power of community still felt by the living for the dead was one of the traumatizing aspects of the Vietnam War.[353] In order for veterans to have peace, they must come to terms with the casualties suffered during their deployment.[354] "God built the grief response into us for the purpose of mentally, emotionally and spiritually processing loss-producing events . . . and helping us move to a state of greater strength, resourcefulness, resilience and faith."[355]

Since memorial services will have already been conducted in the theatre of war for any casualties sustained by a unit, the "roll-call" should not appear to be a second memorial service. Instead, since the dead arrive home before the living in modern war[356], the "roll-call" is meant to establish that all the members of a unit, both the living and the dead, have returned to their native land. An illustration of this principle is Exodus 13:19 where Moses brought Joseph's mummy with the army as the people of Israel returned to the land God promised to Abraham. As noted in *Achilles in Vietnam*, there can be a "resuscitative function" in the nephesh of a person when he or she feels like the dead are "present" again, even though it is just a mental exercise.[357]

The mission of the third day is to address the wound of moral injury. In the previous chapter of this study it was noted that there is a connection between "moral injury" and PTSI. [358] "Moral injury may also lead to emotional numbing (detachment, disinterest, and difficulty experiencing pleasure)."[359] In *Odysseus in America,* Jonathan Shay discusses a particular factor in military moral injury: command climate.[360] In a separate essay Shay names the nephesh injury perpetrated by superiors upon their subordinates as "leadership malpractice."[361] Shay explains how "leadership malpractice leads to moral injury:

> My current most precise (and narrow) definition has three
> parts: moral injury is present when (1) there has been a
> betrayal of what's right (2) by someone who holds legitimate
> authority (3) in a high-stakes situation. When all three are
> present, moral injury is present and the body codes it in much
> the same way it codes physical attack.

The officers of the detachment for the Midian campaign in Numbers 31 meet Shay's standard for "leadership malpractice." The military has their own word for what these leaders did. It is called "mutiny." *The Manual for Courts-Martial* defines "mutiny" as "any person who, in concert with other persons and with intent to usurp or override lawful military authority, refuses to obey orders or otherwise do his duty."[362] Moses looked at the baggage train of the returning warriors and then he chastised ". . . the officers of the army, the captains over thousands and captains over hundreds, who came from the battle" (Nu 31:14). These officers had failed to follow Moses' orders and had put the very survival of their unit and the nation at risk merely for sexual favors (Nu 31:15-16). Other examples of "mutiny" in Scripture are: Saul's failure to destroy the Amalekites (1Sa 15:9); Joab's execution of Absalom (2Sa 18:14); and King Jehoash's failure to properly execute the orders of the prophet Elisha (2Ki 13:18-19). Each of these infractions had an impact on the soldiers under these mutinous leaders.

Earlier in this study the assertion was made that the Benim Korah in Psalm 44: 11-18 charge God with leadership malpractice. In the next verse the Benim Korah tell God that the result is death-shadow. This reaction to moral injury is common in veterans of modern wars: "Where soldiers once viewed God as the awesome and transcendent force active in the world, they may now see . . .not everyone is playing by these rules, and God has failed to bring about justice in the world"[363] Professor Michael Linden and his colleagues at the Charité in Berlin have suggested the stress reaction to moral injury be named "Post-Traumatic Embitterment Disorder."[364] Any bitterness towards God and/or people should be addressed during the "mission" of the third "day". The Bible tells us "Let no one become like a bitter plant that grows up and causes many troubles with its poison" (Heb 12:15). One of those troubles is PTSI.

The fourth "day" of the modern cleansing rite should be a separation process for the veterans from illicit sexual relations. An additional feature of the death-shadow decontamination for civilians (Nu 19), and death-shadow decontamination for military personnel (Nu 31) is renouncing sexual impropriety. In Moses' military version, veterans have to be separated from illicit sexual relations represented by some of their captives (Nu 31:15-16). The instigator of these unorthodox relationships was Balaam, a Midianite priest, who attempted to defeat Israel through sexual acts to Baal Peor (Nu 25:1-2; Nu31:16). Balaam's toxic sexual recipe is also condemned in the Final Covenant (2Pe 2:14-15).

It was sexual relations outside the ordinances of God that the veterans of Moabite campaign were being cleansed from rather than the women themselves. The Mosaic quarantine treated Moabite women with no sexual experience in the same manner as the soldiers of Israel and recognized that they were on the road to integration into the society as brides. No similar wave of war-brides has been part of America's veterans return from current wars.[365] In fact, there is almost no way for U.S. forces to have personal relations with the local people, sexual or otherwise.[366] There is however an environment of pornography among U.S. forces engaged in these modern wars.[367] The Greek word *porneuo* (πορνευω) that forms half of the English word "pornography" is also the root word for the injunction against "fornication" in Acts 15:20 where the early Church issued the four precepts of Mosaic Law still applicable to Christians.[368] According to *Strong's* πορνευω means to, ". . . indulge unlawful lust (of either sex)."[369] Pornography not only impacts a person's ability to connect with God in a civilian setting,[370] but it is also a common form of self-medication for the person suffering from PTSI.[371] For these reasons and the example from Numbers 31 separating a warrior from pornography and any other type of sexual impurity should be included as part of a veterans re-integration.

Another aspect of the military version of the death-shadow decontamination ritual not found in the civilian purification rite is the sharing of spoils. In Numbers 31:26-30, the veterans gave half their spoils to the people who stayed behind, and both parts of the community made an offering to God. This study suggests the mission for the fifth "day" is "spoiling". This term is a deliberate double entendre. The Bible makes clear that what returning warriors do with their spoils has a profound impact on their relationship with God and their fellow citizen. In Genesis 14, the first war narrative of the Hebrew Scriptures, Abraham gives a tenth of his spoils to the priest Melchizedek. This act of "spoiling" becomes one of the arguments used in the Epistle to the Hebrews to support the supremacy of Jesus' priesthood over the Levitical priesthood (Heb 7:6). In contrast to this positive example, King Saul did not deal properly with the spoils from his campaign against the Amalekites and this act "spoiled" God's opinion of Saul (1Sa 15:11).

"Spoiling" is a way to share the benefits and the liabilities of war between those who went to war and those who stayed behind another. King David made the sharing of spoils between those who bore the burden of battle and those who remained behind a policy in the army of Israel (1Sa 30:24). One of the "spoils" of war is the honor given to veterans (1Sa 18:7). One of the liabilities is shame (2Sa 19:3). Jonathan Shay concludes "The earliest inventors of democratic politics invented equal citizen honor [between warriors and civilians] . . . as the necessary psychological and social substructure for democracy."[372] In the context of death-pollution, "spoiling" allows veterans to see that the civilian society that sent the military to war also has a shared need to be washed.

The "mission" of the sixth day is cleansing by "mouth-wash." The need for "mouthwash" is based on the original reason Moses stopped the veterans of Israel from entering the civilian population with the Midianite captives. These captives spoke dirty "words" (דבר)[373] put in their mouth by their religious leader (Nu 31:16). For this verse the King James Version translates their impurity as Balaam's "counsel." Moses was referring to an earlier narrative, when the Moabites used their counsel to persuade the Israelites to pollute themselves by sexual acts for the benefit of Baal Peor (Nu 25:2-3). The Christian Scriptures contain a parallel account of Balaam's counsel in 2 Peter 2:14-15, ". . . they are children of cursing, whose hearts are well used to bitter envy; Turning out of the true way, they have gone wandering in error, after the way of Balaam, the son of Beor . .." (BBE) Both of these passages suggest Balaam's "words" are a danger to the individual and the community.

Modern therapists recognize that "words" have a significant impact on persons suffering from PTSI.[374] "[G]iven the nature of human language, the description and evaluation of the trauma itself can be aversive."[375] This statement is nothing more than a modern restatement of Proverbs 18:12, "Death and life are in the power of the tongue, and those who love it shall eat the fruit of it." In order to protect their families many veterans choose not to speak about their war experiences. Sometimes it is not the content of the recollection that is considered risky, but rather the vocabulary that has become part of the narrative. A manifestation of this reticence can be found in mass media outlets who are censoring their reports from the wars in Iraq and Afghanistan because of the cursing of the warriors.[376] Parachurch ministries Military Churches are warned that returning veterans may include long strings of profanity when speaking of their recent deployments.[377] Even military chaplains recognize that war-zone vocabulary is not what the people back home would be comfortable with in their churches.[378]

The seventh day, which is the conclusion of the rite would be the most appropriate time to "wash" the veterans of death-shadow as the last ceremonial act before reintegration into the community. This was the final stage of Moses' quarantine (Nu 31:24). Significantly the last ritual Jesus conducted for his disciples was a "wash" ministry before they went off to combat (Jn 13:12;13:37-38). Jesus knew that his disciples would be tainted by death-shadow because of the swordfight in the Garden of Gethsemane. Jesus reminds Peter that one dynamic of all combat is the possibility of death (Mt 26:52). Jesus foretold Peter that in the process of Jesus' death, Peter would violate his conscience (Mt 26:34; Mk 14:30; Lk 22:34; Jn 13;38).[379] All the disciples demonstrated a stress reaction to the battle and ran for their lives (Mt 26:56; Mk 14:50).

Jesus had tried to caution these men that they would behave this way when they lost their leader (Mt 26:31; Mk 14:23). This warning points to the significance of Jesus rinsing all the disciples' feet and telling them, "You do not know what I do now, but you shall know hereafter " (Jn 13:7). His prophecy was just hours before their feet took them to a battlefield and then to a place of death. This was not the only prophylactic action Jesus took prior to his death for necessities that would be required after his execution. At the house of Simon the Leper a woman pours expensive scented oil on Jesus (Mt 26:7; Mk 14:3). The disciples do not understand what the woman is doing so Jesus explains, "She has come beforehand to anoint My body for the burying" (Mk 14:8). Jesus knows that when the time comes for his corpse to receive this ministry, his disciples will have run away, worried about their own skin (Mt 26:31; Mk 14:27).

The Foot and Death

"Foot" cleansing as a prerequisite to God's presence has a long tradition in God's covenant with his people. When Moses met God at the burning bush, God commanded Moses to take off his sandals so that he would not bring uncleanness onto holy ground (Ex 3:5). This sanitizing action revealed that "moral uncleanness" is not the only barrier to communing with God. Another implication of this pre-Sinai sanction is that the barrier of "uncleanness" was already in existence prior to the giving of the Law. Peter learned that this barrier still existed even in the age of the Messiah when Jesus told Peter he would be cut-off if Jesus did not wash his feet (Jn 13:8). In Mark Jesus teaches that the "foot" should be cut-off if it causes a person to offend God rather than the person be cut-off from God (Mk 9:45).

The offense of the "foot" that is at the heart of this study is "walking in the valley of death-shadow" which is metaphor for exposure to a deadly environment. Numbers 19:14 says that whoever walks into a building that contains a dead body is unclean. In the First

Covenant this uncleanness has to be washed off with a slurry made of heifer ashes or the person will not be able to enter God's presence (Nu 19:20). Even if a person walks up on a dead body on a battle field, or steps on a grave, this person is unclean in the eyes of God (Num 19:16). This offense is what Jesus alludes to when he condemns some of his audience in Luke 11:44, "For you are like unseen tombs and the men walking above are not aware of them."
Even in the Final Covenant death-shadow is associated with the feet.

Jesus told his disciples before they went into battle that "He who is bathed has no need except to wash *his* feet, but is clean every whit" (John 13:10). The author of Hebrews says that Jesus' blood has become the new solvent for works of death (Heb 9:14). In order to accomplish the mission of the 7th "day" of death-shadow purification these two injunctions must be connected. This study suggests that the feet of veterans be sprinkled with the contents of the communion cup. This may seem odd at first because Jesus did not sprinkle his disciples' feet and no mention is made of the liquid he used but water is the traditional assumption. Yet water alone was insufficient to sanitize a person from death-shadow under the First Covenant, and the Final Covenant says that Jesus' blood is the new solvent for death in its various forms (Heb 9:13-14).

Despite the desire among Christians to operate exactly as Jesus did, the truth is that not even in the days of the first disciples did they minister using the same techniques that their teacher utilized. The Gospel of John records that Jesus did not baptize anyone (John 4:2). Rather it was his disciples that performed this ministry. After his resurrection Jesus insisted the disciples carry on this ministry (Matt 28:19 ;Mark 16:16). Jesus also imparted the Holy Spirit in a different manner than his disciples. He "breathed" the Holy Spirit on them (John 20:22). In contrast his disciples imparted the Holy Spirit with the laying on of hands (Acts 8:17 and 19:6). In Jesus' final pre-ascension instructions in the Gospel of Mark, he tells them that, "they will take up serpents; and if they drink any deadly thing, it will not hurt them" (Mark 16:18). Scripture does not record Jesus doing either of these two "signs", but the apostle Paul took up a poisonous serpent after his shipwreck with no ill effect (Acts 28:3). The point of these examples is to suggest that "washing" the feet of death-shadowed veterans with a sprinkling from the Communion cup should not be ignored merely because Jesus did not use this technique. Instead this sprinkling should be seen as the application of 1 Peter 1:2 where A. M. Stibbs says, "The 'sprinkling of the blood' in the case of Christ's sacrifice means the extension to the persons sprinkled of the value and benefits of the death of which it is the token."[380]

CHAPTER 7

Conclusion

An Analytical Investigation Leading to a Proposal for a Christian Purification Rite to Minister to Veterans Suffering from Posttraumatic Stress Injury.

Implications of the Findings

1. This study has shown that America has an ever-increasing population of returning veterans. Almost two million men and women have participated in the wars in Afghanistan and Iraq. The Rand Corporation projects that 26 % of the veterans of these wars will have Posttraumatic Stress Injury. If the Rand prediction is accurate, approximately 500,000 men and women will be returning to America carrying this wound to their nephesh. This half-million populace will join an existing veteran compilation from previous wars whom carry the wound of PTSI. Forty percent of these veterans will seek help from a clergy person.[381] The implication is that some of these veterans will also seek relief from among the ministries of the Church.

2. This study showed that PTSI is a wound of war that effects both body and nephesh. The study also showed that Jesus and his disciples were in combat. Before and after their exposure to death, Jesus attended to the wounds of body and nephesh produced by a deadly environment. The implication is that Jesus expects his disciples to continue to attend to the needs of wounded veterans.

3. This study found two types of impurities that separate a person from God. One type of impurity is sin and the other type is death-exposure. Despite the Scriptural teachings that show veterans come home from war needing to be cleansed of death-exposure, this study found the response of the Church has been to treat PTSI as if it were caused by sin. As was the case with Abraham's nephew Lot who received the wrong type of ministry for his exposure to death, and thus later developed PTSI, the implication is that modern veterans are being put

at risk of further harm by the malpractice of the Church.

4. This study found that many persons in the Hebrew Scripture had symptoms that corresponded to the clinical requirements for PTSI. [382] Modern clinicians have observed that people with PTSI frequently have trouble with their faith. The Hebrew Scriptures confirm that exposure to death has a pathological effect on a person's nephesh and their relationship with God. Also contained in these ancient war narratives are the methods used to remove death-exposure as an impediment to their faith. The implication is that there must be a way to remove death-exposure as an impediment to a modern veteran's relationship with God.

5. This study found that in the Hebrew Scriptures is a word that corresponds to the first clinical requirement of PTSI, exposure to a deadly situation, and this word is used in ways that match complimentary matrixes found in the works of Jonathan Shay and Robert Lifton. These two men are respected authorities on trauma reactions in people. The Biblical word for PTSI is צלמות which is translated in this study as "death-shadow." God revealed to the prophet Isaiah that one day people suffering from צלמות could be cured by a "great light" (Is 9:2). When the time came for the fulfillment of Isaiah's prophecy, God revealed to Zechariah, the father of John the Baptist, and to the author of Matthew's Gospel who this "great light" is that was the remedy for ותצלמ (Mt 4:16; Lk 1:79). The remedy revealed in Scripture for צלמות is Jesus, "the light of the world" (Jn 8:14). In a living demonstration of Isaiah 9:2, a man with military associations and who had death-shadow is returned to his right mind by Jesus (Mk 5:15). The implication is that Jesus is still the answer for death-shadow.

6. This study found that the Scriptures contain twelve types of ministry for veterans. This study also found that the modern Church practices nine of the twelve types. Of the three ministries not practiced today, the Ark ministry and the Holocaust ministry are impossible to re-instate because of the destruction of the Temple and the loss of the Ark. The third non-existent ministry, Wash ministry, could still be practiced by Christians because the components for its conduct exist in the Church today. The implication is that God's people could re-

instate the Wash ministry for today's veterans.

7. This study found that in the First Covenant the remedy for death-exposure was being washed with the slurry from a red cow's ashes (Nu 19:9). In the Final Covenant the wash is done using the blood of Jesus (Heb 9:13-14). Christians have had access to his blood since the cup of the Last Supper (Lk 22:20; 1Co 11:25). No other access to Jesus' blood for ministry on earth is found in Scripture. This study found that no ministry or rite currently exists to purify veterans from death-exposure using the blood of Jesus. The implication is that purification from death-exposure is possible using the contents of the cup from the Lord's Supper.

8. This study found that Moses conducted a Wash ceremony for his veterans that dealt with a medley of other issues that veterans face when they have to re-integrate to civilian life. These issues were: grief; illicit sexual practices; leadership malpractice; inappropriate language; tithing; and death-exposure. Moses used veterans from previous campaigns to supervise the garrison he established outside the main camp in order to deal with these issues. This study illustrated how the issues Moses' veterans faced are still carried home from deployments by U.S. veterans. Even the manner that Moses used to establish the garrison is recommended by experts in the field of healing liturgy. The implication is that Moses' example could be a model for Wash ministry to modern veterans.

Applications of the Findings

1. Since it should be expected that some of the 500,000 veterans wounded with PTSI will make their way to the doors of the Church, the people of the Church should be familiar with the signs of this injury. It is also important that people in Church know where help for this injury can be obtained.

2. Since Jesus attended to the physical and nephesh injuries of battle and exposure to death, his disciples need to be ready to do the same. In John 14:12 Jesus told his disciples "He who believes on Me, the works that I do he shall do also, and greater works than these he shall

do, because I go to My Father."

3. Since veterans who receive the wrong treatment for any injury do not heal as quickly as those persons who receive the proper therapy, the Church needs to quit treating PTSI as if it was caused by sin since its source is from another spiritual force.

4. Since death-exposure is shown in the First Covenant and in the Final Covenant to be an impediment to faith, and this negative effect on faith is documented even by secular studies, the Church needs to re-align its theology and practices to account for this fact.

5. Since the Biblical term "death-shadow" (צלמות) appears to have all the characteristics associated with clinical term "Post Traumatic Stress Injury", the Church needs to adopt this term for its ministry to returning warriors. By having a separate term for ministry to this injury there would be no confusion that the Church was offering a clinical service, or claiming medical expertise. A "faith" term implies a "faith" solution.

6. Since Wash ministry is the preferred solution for death-exposure in returning warriors, each local church should be familiar with how to conduct this ministry.

7. Since Jesus' blood has replaced the original liquid in the Wash ministry, the Church should use this liquid to purify veterans of death-exposure. Jesus gave the contents of the cup at the Lord's Supper as his blood, thus providing the Church with the resource necessary to conduct the Wash ministry.

8. Since none of the warriors of the Mosaic period are ever tagged by scholars as exhibiting signs of PTSI, and this despite the bloody campaign of extermination against the Midianites, it may be assumed that Moses' quarantine was effective in cleansing his veterans of death-exposure and in dealing with other post-deployment issues. If the Church were to implement a ministry based on the Mosaic model, the Church might be able to shrink the vast pool of veterans who suffer from this injury and prevent a repeat of the aftermath of the Vietnam War.

Further Study

1. Many other professions besides the military are exposed to death and deadly situations. Further study is needed to adapt the Wash ministry for Ambulance Crews, Police, Fire Departments and other vocations with a high incidence of PTSI.

2. Ordinary citizens also experience traumatic situations, like rape or natural disasters, and carry the wound of PTSI. The Church needs to study how to cleanse these people of their death-shadow in a manner that models Jesus.

3. An examination should be made of all ministries that reconcile a person with God in order to see if culpability is the only impediment the ministry seeks to alleviate. Since death-exposure is a non-culpable impediment to God's presence, the Church needs to explore forms of reconciliation that do not necessarily contain confession.

Appendix A

Proposed Booklet

for a

WARRIOR WASH RETREAT

Introduction:

The first Christian to see combat action was Peter in the Garden of Gethsemane. Many millions of Christ-followers have been involved in armed conflict since that initial battle.

Secular experts estimate that at least one in five U.S. service members will return from supporting combat operations in Afghanistan and Iraq with Posttraumatic Stress Injury (PTSI).[383] An unknown number will come back to their native land carrying other types of war pollution in their soul.

Unlike some other religions, Christianity does not have a way to decontaminate its members from the toxic effects of war in their soul. I know this because I am a pastor and a military chaplain. I also share a common characteristic with a growing number of Americans: I have come home from war more than once. On each occasion it has been difficult to reconnect with my family, my community and with God.

This booklet is an attempt to provide a way for the Christian Church to decontaminate their veterans in order to facilitate the reintegration of these warriors back into their church and their community.

Welcome the Warrior Home

Jesus is not only the Son of God, he is "a priest forever in the order of Melchizedek." (Psalm 110:4) Scripture records that Melchizedek conducted the first retreat for veterans. He met Abraham's militia returning from war and conducted a service for them in the Valley of the Kings (Gen 14:18-20). Jesus also had a ministry to military personnel. The Gospels record a request from a commanding officer to Jesus, "Just give the order, and my servant will get well."[384] The Centurion recognized the parallel between the authority of Jesus and the structure of military life. Jesus honored the centurion's faith and healed his dependent in the military manner requested by the officer.

Ministry to veterans should contain the orderliness that epitomizes military life. For a warrior-purification activity, the best scriptural model to establish this order comes from the time Moses had to decontaminate his veterans. In Numbers 31, Moses established a garrison outside the rest of the community. He had veterans from previous wars greet the returning warriors. Moses then gave instructions for the veterans to address several sub-categories of war-contamination. These were: (1) mutiny; (2) spoiling; (3) grief; (4) illicit sexual relations; and (5) cursing. After these issues were addressed, the warriors were ready to be cleansed from (6) "works of death."

The most practical way for the Christian community to replicate this "camp outside the camp" is to set aside a weekend retreat hosted by veterans of previous deployments. After this "garrison" or ministry space has been established, the retreat staff can follow an agenda that parallels the one established by Moses. Of course, allowances should be made for the ways these five veterans' issues present themselves in modern warriors.

The Talks

This program for warrior decontamination consists of a series of presentations prior to the final cleansing act. Each presentation represents an aspect of the Israelite camp in Numbers 31. Since each presentation is followed by a small group activity, the room that hosts these presentations should be set up in such a way as to allow the veterans to be seated in their small groups. Whether this means groups sitting around tables, or in conversation circles, the point is to minimize the time and energy needed to transition to small group activities.

Plenary Session Presenters

The plenary session describes the time when one presenter addresses the whole assembly. Whether one person makes all the presentations, or each topic has a separate presenter, the person who speaks at the plenary sessions needs a solid grounding on the subject of their presentation. Besides the Scriptural examples listed with each activity, and the suggested reading list at the end of this booklet, the presenter should research Department of Defense websites and other sources to inform their presentation. Whenever possible the presenter should personalize the subject matter from their own experience. Each presentation should be 10-15 minutes in duration.

Small Group Leaders

After each plenary presentation the small groups get to work. The Small Group Leader (SGL) guides the discussion for their veterans. The SGL should be a veteran of at least one previous deployment. The ideal SGL should be from the same branch of service and have experienced a deployment to the same part of the world. The SGL is meant to be more of a moderator than a preacher in this process.

Small Groups

Moses' army was a national military force, but it was comprised of tribal units.[385] The "garrison" for the veterans' retreat should be organized in a similar fashion with the whole group also divided into smaller units. Whenever possible, warriors who deployed together should not be placed in the same small group. This allows for each individual to process their own war experience.

The First Talk

The first goal is to finish establishing the "garrison." This is the shortest of the presentations. The presenter should insure the groups are sitting together and have identified their leader. Any last minute details should be addressed at this time. The presenter should explain the process to be followed for the presentations, such as the schedule, bathroom breaks and other organizational information.

After the opening prayer, the presenter should introduce himself/herself. The purpose of the introduction is to personalize the presenter and establish their credentials with the group. Since the goal of this first presentation is for the members of the small group to get to know the other members of their "tribe", the presenter for the plenary session need not use the full 10 or 15 minutes that are allotted for the other five presentations.

The Scripture reading for this activity is Numbers 2:1-34. It is suggested that a contemporary translation of the Bible be used for this particular narrative. After the scripture has been read, the small groups begin their work.

Activity #1 Making a "tribe".

Small Group Leader (SGL) Introduction:

Briefly provides biographical details like work history, family status, and prior military service.

Member Introductions

Each answers the question: Who are you, where did you serve? Where are you now?

SGL prompts further information:

> Who is married? Who has children? Who is single? How many tours have you done? What was the hardest part? What was the best part?

> Additional Information- If time permits have group pair off. Each person will interview the other person in order to gain enough information to introduce this person to the group. Suggested questions are: What are their hobbies, favorite teams, home state, vegetables they don't like, and whether they have ever sang karaoke or other unorthodox ice-breakers.

The Second Talk

Scripture Reading: Joshua 24:25-33; Matt 14:3-13a; and John 19:38-42

Unresolved grief causes issues in some veterans for decades after they leave the battlefield. Moses dealt with this issue by conducting a roll call to make sure no one had been left on the battlefield.[386] Some veteran organizations have made the MIA[387] issue, which was the failure to bring everyone home from Vietnam, a central tenet of their lobbying efforts to the national government. In current conflicts, it is not the failure to bring all service members home that needs to be addressed, but rather the disappointment experienced by veterans when they did not return from the war as a complete unit.

The purpose of the third presentation is to examine who and what was lost during the veteran's deployment. The presenter should not turn this session into a second (or 3rd) memorial service for the fallen warriors from the units represented by the veterans. Instead the presenter should set the stage for the small groups to explore what each unit lost when a member was subtracted through death or transfer. This can be a professional observation like the unit's firepower was decreased, or a more personal memory like the platoon lost its joker or internet hog.

Suggested readings for the presenter are: Jonathan Shay's *Odysseus in America: Combat Trauma and the Trials of Homecoming*, p.76-85 and *Achilles in Vietnam: Combat Trauma and the Undoing of Character*, p. 39-68. Also recommended is familiarity with the tradition of the Doolittle Raiders Goblets.
(see http://www.doolittleraider.com/the_goblets.htm.)
The presenter and Small Group Leaders should also be familiar with Gen 50:25—26; Ex 13:19; and Numbers 14, particularly verses 28-39.

Activity #2: Bringing Everyone Home

The goal of this activity is to let the veteran participate in an aspect of the grief process that was formerly denied to him/her.

> For the first Scripture SGL introduces group to the main participants: Jacob, Joseph, Joshua, Eliezer.
>
> Does your family have funeral traditions? What are they?
>
> How do these traditions help your family cope with loss?
>
> Have you ever been an escort or participant in a military funeral? To process the second narrative, SGL introduces John the Baptist, Nicodemus and Joseph of Arimathea
>
> How do you think John's disciples felt when they only received partial remains of their leader?
>
> Why did Joseph and Nicodemus process Jesus' remains rather than his disciples?
>
> Did you experience either incomplete "remains" or "absentee" handling of the losses in your unit?

This session should be closed with members standing for the playing of Taps.

The Third Talk

The next presentation on the agenda should deal with the effects of mutiny. *The Manual for Courts-Martial* defines "mutiny" as "any person who, in concert with other persons and with intent to usurp or override lawful military authority, refuses to obey orders or otherwise do his duty."[388] The leaders of Moses' army had disobeyed orders and enriched themselves by plundering the enemy.[389] Modern psychologists recognize that when military leaders commit breaches of the moral code, their subordinates are vulnerable to suffer Posttraumatic Stress Injury at a later date.[390]

To prepare for this session, the presenter should read Jonathan Shay, *Achilles in Vietnam: Combat Stress and the Undoing of Character* (New York: Scribner,1994) pages 3-21 and Brett T. Litz, et al, "Moral Injury and Moral Repair: A Preliminary Model and Intervention Strategy," in *Clinical Psychology Review* 29 (2009) 695—706.

Scripture Reading: 2 Sam 17:1-23 and Matt 26: 36-56

Activity #3 Mutiny and Me

For discussing the first narrative SGL introduces group to David, Hushai, Absalom, and Ahithophel. (SGL should be familiar with 2 Sam 14 thru 16)

Discussion:

Was a moral breach committed in the first narrative?

Why did Ahithophel take his course of action?

Was Absalom responsible for Ahithophel's death?

Did any incident like this happen in your unit?

For discussing the second narrative SGL introduces group to

Peter, James, John, and Judas, (SGL should be familiar with Matt 26:1-35 and 69-75; John 12:1-9; Mark 3:13-19) :

Who is unfaithful in this narrative?

Why does Judas change sides?

Why does Peter choose violence?

Who was more unfaithful to Jesus? Judas or the other three

How have you dealt with incidents like this when you were deployed?

Was there a time when you felt betrayed by your unit leadership? Did you ever betray their trust?

Participants in the small group should be encouraged to take responsibility for any breach of authority they committed that hurt others. More importantly, the participants are encouraged to forgive their leaders for any betrayal of trust that harmed the veteran. Close this activity with the group saying the Lord's Prayer. Before they begin SGL should remind the group that this prayer was the example Jesus modeled for his disciples. Draw attention to the fact it contains the connection of God's forgiveness and human forgiveness.

The Fourth Talk

Scripture Readings: Gen 29:16-35; 2 Sam 11:1-17; Matt 5:27-32

In Moses' army, the warriors brought back "Moabite women" who represented illicit sexual relations that threatened the Israelite community.[391] Modern veterans also are exposed to a wide range of sexual encounters that threaten American culture. These enticements range from internet pornography to inappropriate relationships within the unit. No matter the source, the resulting loss of intimacy between veterans and their spouses is a significant factor in the high divorce and suicide rate among U.S. forces. Restoring purity to military marriages and relationships would help preserve both veterans and society.

Presenters and SGL's should be familiar with both Department of Defense "Returning from a War Zone" pamphlets listed in the "Suggested Reading" section of this booklet. Many civilian studies on the harmful effect of pornography, adultery, and prostitution are also available. One or more should be consulted before this activity.

The presenter's task is to show veteran's how using substitutes will not only endanger intimacy but put at risk everything the service members sacrificed to preserve.

Activity #4: To highlight "substitutes" in relationships

Why was Jacob more attracted to Leah?

Did having more children increase or decrease the physical attractiveness of Leah?

What factors made Bathsheba attractive to David?

Does Uriah's behavior towards Bathsheba suggest intimacy issues? Did this make it possible for David to seduce Bathsheba?

Is the intense emotional bond formed during deployment a threat to marital relationships?

Is pornography a violation of Matt 5:27-32?

How does the presence of both genders in a unit make it difficult to "pluck it out" (Matt 5:20) if inappropriate feelings have taken place?

This activity should conclude with the SGL giving to each group member a new, white pillow-case with the injunction from Heb 13:4, "Let marriage be kept honorable in every way, and the marriage bed undefiled. For God will judge those who commit sexual sins, especially those who commit adultery."

The Fifth Talk

Scripture Readings: 2 Sam 20:14—22; Matt 10:34-42

An unusual issue that should be addressed in this retreat is "spoiling." In a military context "spoiling" is when participants in a war keep all the spoils to themselves. God commanded Moses to make sure the spoils of war were distributed to the Israelite civilians as part of the warrior quarantine.[392] King David made the sharing of spoils between those who bore the burden of battle and those who remained behind a policy in the army of Israel.[393] In the modern context, the "spoils" are not items of value taken from the enemy. This practice is largely prohibited under the Geneva Conventions of War and the U.S. Uniform Code of Military Justice.[394] Rather, in the context of war-pollution, "spoiling" applies when veterans do not impute to their civilian counterparts the full consequences of the military actions the veteran participated in during their deployment

The cleansing of returning veterans requires the service members to first share their war trophies with the citizens of their community. In this final activity prior to the Warrior Wash, the presenter needs to stress the military/civilian alliance that is not only a part of American democracy but is a Biblical principle. . In God's economy, and especially in our form of government, both glory and tragedy belong equally to the veteran and their civilian counterpart.

Presenter should also draw attention to the fickleness of public

120

opinion towards warriors, both in the Bible and in recent history. In order to balance the presentation, the presenter should also make veterans aware of the situations in other countries (i.e. Egypt and Turkey) where the military has cultural supremacy.

At some point in the presentation the group should be presented with the facts of a military success and a military blunder. While future events may present better examples, it is suggested that Seal Team Six's operation against Osama Bin Laden be used as a military success, and the death by friendly-fire of Army Ranger Pat Tillman be used as a military blunder. This helps the small group leaders with the work they have to do.

Activity #5: To help veterans share "the spoils" of war.

Did you read your hometown newspaper while deployed?

Have you ever voted while deployed? In what way did you participate in your community while deployed? Whose responsibility is that?

What kind of a word is "spoils"?

What types of souvenirs do veterans bring home from war?

Which of these things are not popular among civilians?

Have veterans benefits changed since the GWOT began?

Has a stranger ever thanked you for your service? What did you say to them? Have you ever thanked a civilian for sending you on deployment?

Should civilians get some of the credit for the killing of Osama Bin Laden? Should they get some of the blame for killing Pat Tillman?

Does God allow a veteran to bless a civilian with the spiritual "spoils" of their service?

This activity should finish with civilians from the local community receiving a campaign token from each small group. The civilian recipients should be invited to stay and participate in the warrior purification service.

The Sixth Talk

Scripture Reading: Prov 18:19-2; James 3:5-18

The "mission" of the sixth day is to not "curse". Cursing is the original reason Moses stopped the veterans of Israel from entering the civilian population with the Midianite captives. These captives spoke dirty "words" (דבר[395]) put in their mouth by their religious leader (Nu 31:16). For this verse the King James Version translates their impurity as Balaam's "counsel." The Christian Scriptures contain this summary of Balaam's counsel in 2 Peter 2:14-15, ". . . they are children of cursing, whose hearts are well used to bitter envy; Turning out of the true way, they have gone wandering in error, after the way of Balaam, the son of Beor . .." (BBE) Both of these passages suggest Balaam's "words" are a danger to the individual and the community.

Sometimes it is the vocabulary is risky to the community. A manifestation of this reticence can be found in mass media outlets who are censoring their reports from the wars in Iraq and Afghanistan because of the cursing of the warriors.[396] Para-church ministries Military Churches are warned that returning veterans may include long strings of profanity when speaking of their recent deployments.[397] Even military chaplains recognize that war-zone vocabulary is not what the people back home would be comfortable with in their churches.[398]

More dangerous to veterans themselves is the way they "curse" themselves for what they feel they should or could have done during the war. In order to protect their families many veterans choose not to speak about their war experiences. Modern therapists recognize that "words" have a significant impact on persons suffering from PTSI.[399] "[G]iven the nature of human language, the description and evaluation of the trauma itself can be aversive."[400] This statement is nothing more than a modern restatement of Proverbs 18:12, "Death and life are in the power of the tongue, and those who love it shall eat the fruit of it." Veterans need to learn to tell their war-story in a way that affirms their life and does not "curse" or speak death over their service.

Activity #6: Mouth Wash

(SGL should be familiar with Balaam's ministry in Num 22-24, and his death in Num 31:8) Start the lesson by reading Is 6:1-7

> What does it mean to "live among a people of unclean lips?" Does that describe the military?

> Have you ever told somebody not to say something because you were afraid that would make it happen?

> Do you ever describe yourself in a negative way? How about your time in the military? Your deployment?

> Which is worse Posttraumatic Stress Disorder or Posttraumatic Stress Injury? Why?

> Have you ever said anything to your family after deployment that you regretted? What?

> If you insult or make derogatory remarks about the enemy, the opposite sex, your unit or your family, does it make you smaller or larger?

> We are made in the image of God. How does God create?

> Why is Jesus described as the Word? (John 1:1)

This activity ends with each group member being given a travel size bottle of mouth-wash to use later as a symbolic "coal" to cleanse their unclean lips.

The Seventh Talk

Scripture: Num 31: 1-20, Matt 26:47—51 and Matt 27:1-6

The center piece of this veteran purification retreat is being cleansed from an environment of death. In the Hebrew scripture a person became polluted merely by being in an area that contained a corpse.[401] This contamination made it impossible to worship God.[402] Moses did not care whether his veterans had taken an active part in combat or had merely handled laundry items, contact with any aspect of death had to be removed before his veterans could return to the main camp.[403]

The Jewish *Mishnah* calls corpse-pollution the "father of uncleanness." Modern studies have shown exposure to an environment where death is possible can even alter the physical make-up of the brain. In this activity the presenter should make the connection between corpse-pollution in the Biblical worldview and the environment of death that exists during a deployment. The presenter's goal should be to set the stage for the cleansing ceremony at the conclusion of the next presentation.

Presenters and SGL's should read: (1) Edward Tick's *War and the Soul*, p201—216; David Bosworth's "You have Shed Much Blood, and Waged Great Wars': Killing, Bloodguilt, and Combat Stress". Additional Scripture resources are Num 31: 1-18; Rom 13:1—5;

Activity #7: Escaping An Environment of Death

Do you think you have ever touched something that held a dead body? In the U.S.? While deployed?

If God commanded his people to fight, why do they need purification?

Why would the possibility of death in war effect veterans when they return home?

Was Judas a combatant or a non-combatant in the Garden of Gethsemane? Do you think he knew the priests intended to kill Jesus?

Was it fair that the priests' actions tainted Judas' money and prevented it from being accepted in the offering plate? Can other peoples' actions affect your relationship with God?

Is faith sufficient to protect you from combat stress?

Has it been harder to pray or worship since you returned from deployment?

At the conclusion of Activity #7, the small groups should be invited to gather in the main worship area for the Warrior Wash ceremony.

SUGGESTED READING *
Bosworth, David. "You have Shed Much Blood, and Waged Great Wars': Killing, Bloodguilt, and Combat Stress" in *Journal of Religion, Disability & Health,* Vol 12 (3), 2008, p. 236-250

Department of Veterans Affairs pamphlet, " Returning from the War Zone: A Guide for Families of Military Members" at http://www.ptsd.va.gov/public/reintegration/guide-pdf/FamilyGuide.pdf

Department of Veterans Affairs pamphlet, " Returning from the War Zone: A Guide for Military Personnel" at http://www.ptsd.va.gov/public/reintegration/guide-pdf/SMGuide.pdf

Litz, Brett T., Nathan Stein, Eileen Delaney, Leslie Lebowitz, William

P. Nash, Caroline Silva and Shira Maguen, "Moral Injury and Moral Repair: A Preliminary Model and Intervention Strategy," in *Clinical Psychology Review* 29 (2009) 695-706

Shay, Jonathan.
    Odysseus in America: Combat Trauma and the Trials of Homecoming.
    New York: Scribner, 2002.

    Achilles in Vietnam: Combat Trauma and the Undoing of Character.
    New York: Scribner, 1994

Tanielian, Terri and Lisa H. Jaycox. Editors. *The Invisible Wounds of War: Psychological and Cognitive Injuries, Their Consequences, and Services to Assist Recovery.* Santa Monica, CA: Rand Corporation, 2008

Tick, Edward. *War and the Soul: Healing Our Nation's Veterans from Post-Traumatic Stress Disorder.* Wheaton, Illinois: Quest Books, 2005

*(War is a graphic subject. The works listed, with language used, and situations described therein, may not reflect Christian values or be appropriate for all audiences.)

Appendix B

The Warrior Wash- A Sample Order of Service

<u>Invitation to worship</u>: (Responsive Reading from Isaiah 9:2-6)

> **Leader**: The people who went in the dark have seen a great light, and those who were living in the shadow of death, the light is shining.

> **Veterans:** You have made them very glad, increasing their joy. They are glad before you as warriors are glad when they divide the spoils of war.

> **Leader**: For by your hand the yoke on our neck and the rod on our back, even the rod of the task-master, has been broken.

> **Veterans**: For every trampling boot of the warrior and the clothing rolled in blood, will be for burning, food for the fire.

> **Leader:** For to us a child has come, to us a son is given; and the government has been placed in his hands; and he has been named Wise Guide, Strong God, Father forever, Prince of Peace.

<u>Confession and Pardon</u>

> Leader: The Book of Romans tells us that all have sinned and fallen short of the glory of God. In the next few minutes allow God to show you your trespasses. Let us say together the invitation:

> ALL: Search me, O God, and know my heart: Try me, and know my thoughts; And see if there be any wicked way in me, And lead me in the way everlasting.
> (Psalm 139:23—24 ASV)

(After an appropriate time, the Leader says: Hear the words of Christ—Your sins are forgiven.)

A Song or Hymn

Institution of the Lord's Supper

Leader recites:

For I received from the Lord what I also delivered to you, that the Lord Jesus on the night when he was betrayed took bread, and when he had given thanks, he broke it, and said, "This is my body which is for you. Do this in remembrance of me." In the same way also he took the cup, after supper, saying, "This cup is the new covenant in my blood. Do this, as often as you drink it, in remembrance of me." (1 Cor 11: 23-25 ESV)

(A Prayer of Thanksgiving may be said over the elements)

The Lord's Prayer

Our Father who art in heaven, Hallowed be thy name.
Thy kingdom come. Thy will be done on earth, as it is in heaven. Give us this day our daily bread. And forgive us our trespasses, as we forgive those who trespass against us. And lead us not into temptation, but deliver us from evil: For thine is the kingdom, and the power, and the glory, forever. Amen.

Partaking of the Lord's Supper

(The bread and cup are consecrated and distributed)

Invitation to the Warrior Wash:

Leader: Under the Old Covenant a person exposed to an environment of death could not enter God's Tabernacle without being sprinkled with the waters of purification.[404] In the New Covenant this water has been replaced by the blood of Jesus.[405] Veterans returning from war, and civic leaders who commissioned them to walk in the Valley of the Shadow of Death, what are you seeking from your God?

Veterans and Civic leaders: "O God--Behold, you delight in truth in the inward being, and you teach me wisdom in the secret heart. Purge me with hyssop, and I shall be clean; wash me, and I shall be whiter than snow. Let me hear joy and gladness; let the bones that you have broken rejoice. Create in me a clean heart, O God, and renew a right spirit within me."[406]

Scripture Reading   John 13:4-10a

Sprinkling From the Cup

Leader: Hear the words of Jesus, "He who is bathed has need only to have his feet washed and then he is clean all over: and you, my disciples, are clean"

(The veterans come to the front in small groups)

The Worship Leader recites these words as he/she begins the lustration:

"You were chosen according to the purpose of God the Father and were made a holy people by his Spirit, to obey Jesus Christ and be purified by his blood. **May grace and peace be yours in full measure.**" (1 Peter 1:2 GNB)

(The last phrase could be repeated by whoever administers the branch each time a veteran is sprinkled.)

Benediction

Leader: Veterans, you came to this place and said to God, "If you are willing, you can make me clean." Hear the words of Christ, "I am willing, Be thou clean."[407] Amen

Leave this place to enjoy your nation, your family, and the fruits of your sacrifice. May God bless you!

Bibliography

Adsit, Chris. *The Combat Trauma Healing Manual: Christ-centered Solutions for Combat Trauma*. Newport News, VA: Military Ministry Press, 2008.

------, Rahnella Adsit, and Marshele Carter Waddell. *When War Comes Home: Christ-Centered Healing for Wives of Combat Veterans*. Newport News, Virginia: Military Ministry Press, 2008.

Allman, Mark J. *Who Would Jesus Kill: War, Peace and the Christian Tradition*. Winona, Minnesota: Anselm Academic, 2008.

Alpers, Matthew. *The God Part of the Brain: A Scientific Interpretation of Human Spirituality and God*. Naperville, Illinois: Sourcebooks Inc., 2006.

American Psychiatric Association. *Diagnostic and Statistical Manual of Mental Disorders, 4th ed., text rev.* Washington, D.C. : American Psychiatric Association, 2000.

------ "Practice guideline for the treatment of patients with major depressive disorder (revision)." *American Journal of Psychiatry* 157, no. 4 Suppl., (April 2000): 1–45.

Anderson, Herbert. "How Rituals Heal", *Word and World* 30, no. 1 (Winter 2010):1-8.

Bainton, Roland H. *Christian Attitudes Toward War and Peace*. Nashville: Abbingdon Press, 1960.

Barnes, Albert. *Notes on the New Testament*. Edited by Robert Frew. Vol. 1 and 2. Grand Rapids, MI: Baker Book House, 1949.

Beck, Aaron, *A.* John Rush, Brian F. Shaw, and Gary Emery. *Cognitive Therapy of Depression*. New York: The Guilford Press, 1979.

Blau, Joseph L. "The Red Heifer: A Biblical Purification Rite in Rabbinic Literature." *Numen* 14, no.1 (Mar 1967): 70-78.

Boling, Robert G. *The Anchor Bible: Judge.* New York: Doubleday, 1975.

Boscarino, Joseph A. "The Mortality Impact of Combat Stress 30 Years after Exposure: Implications for Prevention, Treatment and Research." in *Combat Stress Injury: Theory, Research, and Management,* edited by Charles R. Figley and William P. Nash, 97-117. New York: Routledge, 2007.

Bosworth, David. "'You have Shed Much Blood, and Waged Great Wars': Killing, Bloodguilt, and Combat Stress." *Journal of Religion, Disability & Health* 12, (3) (2008): 236-250.

Brand, Chad, Charles Draper, and Archie England, eds. *Holman Illustrated Bible Dictionary.* Nashville, Tennessee: Holman Publishing, 2003.

Bremmer, J. Douglas. "Brain Imaging in Anxiety Disorders." *Expert Review Neurotherapeutics* 4, (2) (Mar 2004): 89-98.

------. Neuroimaging studies in post-traumatic stress disorder," *Current Psychiatry Reports* (Aug 2002): 254-263.

Brotzman, Ellis R. "Man and the Meaning of נֶפֶשׁ." *Bibliotheca sacra* 145, no. 580 Oct-Dec 1988: 403.

Brown, Frances, S.R. Driver, and Charles A. Briggs. *The Brown-Driver-Briggs Hebrew and English Lexicon.* Peabody, Massachusetts: Hendrickson Publishers, 1996.

Cole, Darrell. "Just War, Penance and the Church." *Pro Ecclesia* 11, no 3 (Sum 2002): 313-328.

Calpino, Teresa. "The Gerasene Demoniac (Mark 5:1-20): the Pre-Markan Function of the Pericope." *Biblical Research* 53 (2008): 15-23.

Catechism of the Catholic Church: Pocket Edition. London: Geoffrey Chapman, 1995.

Chamberlain, Ken. "The Gadarene Demoniac Finds Wholeness." *Journal of Pastoral Care & Counseling* 61, no 1-2 (Spring-Summer 2007): 134.

Christopher, Paul. *The Ethics of War and Peace: An Introduction to Legal and Moral Issues.* Englewood Cliffs, New Jersey: Prentice Hall Inc, 1994.

Cole, Darrell. "Just War, Penance and the Church." *Pro Ecclesia* 11, no. 3 (Summer 2002): 313-328.

Courson, Jon. *Jon Courson's Application Commentary: Old Testament, vol.*1, *Genesis-Job.* Nashville: Nelson, 2005.

Dana, Rebecca. "@$#&*% Ken Burns! PBS Scrubbing G.I. Mouths With Soap."*New York Observer* (Oct. 2, 2006).

Denton, Donald D., Jr. "Descended Into Hell: Consultation On The Vietnam Experience." *The Journal of Pastoral Care* 41, no. 4. (December 1987): 353-359.

Derrett, J. Duncan M. "Contributions To The Study Of The Gerasene Demoniac." *Journal for the Study of the New Testament* 2 (May 1979): 2-17.

Dorn, Christopher and John Zemmler. "The Invisible Wounds of War: Post-Traumatic Stress Disorder and Liturgy in Conversation." *Call to Worship* 43, no. 2 (2009-2010):1-8.

Douglas, Mary. *Purity and Danger: An Analysis of the Concepts of Purity and Taboo.* New York: Routledge, 1994.

Figley, Charles R. and William P. Nash, eds. *Combat Stress Injury: Theory, Research, and Management.* New York: Routledge, 2007.

Fontana, Alan and Robert Rosenheck, "Trauma, Change in Strength of Religious Faith, and Mental Health Service Use Among Veterans Treated for PTSD." *The Journal of Nervous and Mental Disease* 192, no. 9 (September 2004): 579-584.

Granjo, Paulo. "The Homecomer: Postwar Cleansing Rituals in Mozambique." *Armed Forces & Society* 33, no. 3 (April 2007): 382-395.

Green, J.P. ed. *Modern King James Bible,* Rev. ed. Lafayette, IN: Sovereign Grace Trust Fund, 1990.

Green, Robin. *Only Connect: Worship and Liturgy from the Perspective of Pastoral Care.* London: Darton, Longman and Todd, 1993.

Grenier, Stephane, Kathy Darte, Alexandra Heber, and Don Richardson. "The Operational Stress Injury Social Support Program: A Peer Support Program in   Collaboration between the Canadian Forces and Veterans Affairs Canada," in   *Combat Stress Injury: Theory, Research, and Management,* edited by Charles R. Figley and William P. Nash, 261-293. New York: Routledge, 2007.

Hamer, Rupert. "Faith on the Iraq Frontline; REMEMBER OUR HEROES."*Sunday Mirror* (Nov. 11, 2007).

Hart, Ashley. *An Operators Manual for Combat PTSI: Essays for Coping.* Lincoln, NE: iUniverse.Com, 2000.

Hobbs, T.R. *A Time for War: A Study of Warfare in the Old Testament.* Wilmington, Delaware: Michael Glazier, 1989.

Hunter, Edna J. "The Psychological Effects of Being a Prisoner of War." In *Human Adaptation to Extreme Stress: From the Holocaust to Vietnam,* edited by John P. Wilson, Zev Harel, and Boaz Kahana, 157-170. New York: Plenum Press, 1988.

Iasiello, Louis V. *Jus in Bellum: Key Issues for a Contemporary Assessment of Just Behavior in War,* PhD diss., Salve Regina University, 2003.

Irle, Eva, Mirjana Ruhleder, Claudia Lange, Ulrich Seidler-Brandler, Simone Salzer, Peter Dechent, Godehard Weniger, Eric Leibing, and Falk Leichsenring. "Reduced Amygdalar and Hippocampal Size in Adults with Generalized Social Phobia." *Journal of Psychiatry Neuroscience* 35 (2), (2010):126-131.

Joint Service Committee on Military Justice. *The Manual for Courts-Martial United States.* 2002 edition.

Kime, Patricia. "Leadership's Progress on Suicide Appears to Lag." *Navy Times*, (August 27, 2012).

Lanius, Ruth, C.R. Brewin, J.D. Bremmer, J.K. Daniels, M.J. Friendman, I. Liberzon, A. McFarlane, P.P. Schnurr, L. Shin, M. Stein, and E. Vermetten. "Does Neuroimaging Research Examining the Pathophysiology of Posttraumatic Stress Disorder Require Medication-free Patients?" *Journal of Psychiatry and Neuroscience* 35.2 (March 2010): 80-89.

Litz, Brett T., Nathan Stein, Eileen Delaney, Leslie Lebowitz, William P. Nash, Caroline Silva and Shira Maguen, "Moral Injury and Moral Repair: A Preliminary Model and Intervention Strategy." *Clinical Psychology Review* 29 (2009): 695-706.

Lifton, Robert J. "Understanding the Traumatized Self: Imagery, Symbolization, and Transformation" in *Human Adaptation to Extreme Stress: From Holocaust to Vietnam.* Edited by John P. Wilson, Zev Harel, and Boaz Kahana, 7-32. New York: Plenum Press, 1988.

Lugar, Steven. "Flood, Salt, and Sacrifice: Post Traumatic Stress Disorders in Genesis." *Jewish Bible Quarterly* 38.2 (Apr. 2010): 124.

Madden, Thomas E. "Inventing the Crusades." *First Things* 43 (June/July 2009): 41-44.

Mansfield, Stephen. *The Faith of the American Soldier*. Lake Mary, Florida: Front Line, 2005.

Marmar, Charles R. and Mardi J. Horowitz. "Diagnosis and Phase-Oriented Treatment of Post-Traumatic Stress Disorder." in *Human Adaptation to Extreme Stress: From Holocaust to Vietnam*. Edited by John P. Wilson, Zev Harel and Boaz Kahana, 81-103, New York: Plenum Press, 1988.

McNair, Bruce. "Luther, Calvin and the Exegetical Tradition of Melchisedec." *Review and Expositor* 101 (Fall 2004): 747-761.

McNeill, John T. and Helena M. Gamer. *Medieval Handbooks of Penance*. New York: Columbia University Press, 1938.

Michel, Walter L. "SLMWT, "Deep Darkness" or "Shadow of Death?" *Biblical Research*, 29 (1984): 5-20.

Milgrom, Jacob. "Encroaching on the Sacred: Purity and Polity in Numbers 1-10," *Interpretations* 51.3 (July 1997): 241-253.

------. *The JPS Torah Commentary: Numbers*. Philadelphia: The Jewish Publication Society, 1990.

Montefiore, H.W. *The Epistle to the Hebrews*. London: A & C Black, 1987.

Moore, Bret A. and Greg M. Reger. "Historical and Contemporary Perspectives of Combat Stress and Army Combat Stress Control Team." in *Combat Stress Injury, Theory, Research, and Management*, eds. Charles R. Figley and William P. Nash, 161-181. New York: Routledge, 2007.

Moquin, CDR Neal. "Personal Combat Readiness: Moral, Mental, and Emotional Fitness." a presentation provided to 4th Marine Corps Air Wing. Undated (N.p)

Navy Chaplain Corp, "Combat Operation Stress First Aid." (2009) (N.p.)

Nash, William P. "Combat/Operational Stress Adaptations and Injuries." in *Combat Stress Injury: Theory, Research, and Management,* edited by Charles R. Figley and William P. Nash, 33-63. New York: Routledge, 2007.

------. "The Stressors of War." in *Combat Stress Injury: Theory, Research, and Management,* edited by Charles R. Figley and William P. Nash, 11-31. New York: Routledge, 2007.

Nash, William and Dewleen G. Baker. "Competing and Complementary Models of Combat Stress Injury." in *Combat Stress Injury: Theory Research, and Management,* edited by Charles R. Figley and William P. Nash, 65-94. New York: Routledge, 2007.

National Center for Post-Traumatic Stress Disorder and Walter Reed Army Medical Center. *The Iraq War Clinician Guide,* 2nd Edition, June 2004.

Neusner, Jacob, trans. *The Mishnah: A New Translation.* New Haven, CT: Yale University Press, 1988.

Osborn, Ronald E. "Religious Freedom and the Form of the Church : An Assessment of the Denomination in America." *Lexington Theological Quarterly* 11, no 3 (July, 1976): 85-106.

Organ, Barbara E. "Pursuing Phinehas: A Synchronic Reading." *The Catholic Biblical Quarterly* 63 (2001): 203-218.

Plaut, W. Gunther. *The Torah: A Modern Commentary-Genesis.* New York: The Union of American Hebrew Congregations, 1972.

Pontifical Council for Justice and Peace. *Compendium of the Social Doctrine of The Church.* Washington, D.C.:USCCB Publishing, 2004.

Proctor, John. "Proselytes and Pressure Cookers: The Meaning and Application of Acts 15:20." *International Review of Mission* (Oct. 1, 1996): 469-483.

Ross, Jr., Bobby. "Scripture Tags Offer Hope, Comfort to Soldiers in Iraq." *The Houston Chronicle* (Nov. 16, 2003).

Ramshaw, Elaine. *Ritual and Pastoral Care.* Edited by Don S. Browning. Philadelphia: Fortress Press, 1987.

Rappaport, Roy A. "Ritual Time and Eternity." *Zygon* 27, no 1. (March 1992): 5-30.

Ruth, Peggy Joyce and Angelia Ruth Schum. *Psalm 91: God's Shield of Protection.* Sisters, Oregon: The 1687 Foundation, 2009.

Selby, Gary S. "The Meaning and Function of Συνείδησις in Hebrews 9 and 10" in *Restoration Quarterly* 28, no. 3 (1985-1986): 145-154.

Shay, Jonathan. *Achilles in Vietnam: Combat Trauma and the Undoing of Character.* New York: Scribner, 1994.

------. "Casualties." *Daedalus* 140.3 (2011): 179-188.

------. *Odysseus in America: Combat Trauma and the Trials of Homecoming.* New York: Scribner, 2002.

Sippola, John, Amy Blumenshine, Donald Tubesing, and Valerie Yancy. *Welcome Them Home Help Them Heal: Pastoral Care and Ministry with Service Members Returning from War.* Duluth, Minnesota: Whole Person Associates, 2009.

Songer, Harold S. "A Superior Priesthood: Hebrews 4:14-7:28." in *Review & Expositor* 82, no. 3 (Sum 1985): 345-359.

Stibbs, A. M. *The Meaning of the Word 'Blood' in Scripture,* 3rd ed. London: Tyndale, 1962.

Struthers, William M. *Wired for Intimacy*. Downers Grove, IL: Intervarsity Press, 2009.

Tanielian, Terri and Lisa H. Jaycox, eds. *The Invisible Wounds of War: Psychological and Cognitive Injuries, Their Consequences, and Services to Assist Recovery*. Santa Monica, CA: Rand Corporation, 2008.

Taylor, T. Andrew and Michael E. Sherr. "When Veterans Come Home," *Family and Community Ministries*, 21, no. 3 (Winter 2008): 6-16.

Thayer, Joseph Henry, trans. *A Greek-English Lexicon of the New Testament: Being Grimm's Wilke's Clavis Novi Testamenti*. Grand Rapids, Michigan: Baker Book House, 1977.

Thomas, T.K. "Melchizedek, King and Priest: An Ecumenical Paradigm?". *Ecumenical Review* 52, no. 3 (July 2000): 403-409.

Tick, Edward. *War and the Soul: Healing Our Nation's Veterans from Post-Traumatic Stress Disorder*. Wheaton, Illinois: Quest Books, 2005.

The United Methodist Church. *The Discipline of the United Methodist Church*. Nashville: The United Methodist Publishing House, 2008.

Verkamp, Bernard J. *The Moral Treatment of Returning Warriors in Early Medieval and Modern Times*. Scranton, Pennsylvania: University of Scranton Press, 2006.

------. "Moral Treatment of Returning Warriors in the Early Middle Ages," *Journal of Religious Ethics* 16, no. 2 (Fall 1988): 223-249.

Walser, Robyn, Darrah Westrup, and Steven C. Hayes. *Acceptance & Commitment Therapy for the Treatment of Post-Traumatic Stress Disorder: A Practitioner's Guide to Using Mindfulness & Acceptance Strategies*. Oakland, CA: New Harbinger Publication, June 2007.

Walter Reed Army Institute of Research of the U.S. Army Medical Research and Material Command. *Ten Tough Facts about Combat: And What Leaders Can Do to Mitigate Risk and Build Resilience.* N.p., March 2006.

Wolman, Benjamin and George Stricker, eds, *"Depressive Disorders: Facts Theories, and Treatment Methods.* New York: John Wiley and Sons, 1990.

Wright, David P. "Purification from Corpse-Contamination in Numbers XXXI, 19-24," *Vetus Testamentum* 35, 2 (1985): 213-223.Zanchettin, Leo, ed. "A Sign that Heals." *The Word Among Us* 31, no. 6 (June 2012): 4-9.

Electronic Sources

Banks, Adelle M. "Southern Baptists Convention fighting 'don't ask, don't tell' repeal." *Washington Post.* (June 19, 2010). http://www.washingtonpost.com/wp-dyn/content/article/2010/06/18/AR2010061804890.html (accessed Mar 11, 2011).

Bender, Laura, "An Order for Welcoming Service Members Returning from War." (May 2007). http://www.gbhem.org/site/apps/nlnet/content2.aspx?c=lKSL3POLvF&b=5079785&ct=4969667 (Accessed May 18, 2011).

------. "An Order for Blessing Service Members Deploying to War." http://www.gbhem.org/site/apps/nlnet/content2.aspx?c=lsKSL3POLvF&b=5079785&ct=4969669 (accessed June 3, 2012).

Bidwell, Paula. "Native American Sweat Lodge 'Inipi' Ceremony." *Ezine Articles.* http://ezinearticles.com/?Native-American-Sweat-Lodge-Inipi-Ceremony&id=2089226 (accessed Aug 2, 2011).

Bright, Bill. *"The 4 Spiritual Laws."* Orlando, Florida: New Life Publications, 1965. http://4laws.com/laws/english/flash/ (accessed June 9, 2012).

Cardiff University. "Confronting Trauma Directly Most Effective for PTSD." *NewsRx* (May 17, 2005) http://www.newsrx.com/pdf_articles.php?accessID=6a081a0e7 61b47fd292334607b7f75a9 (accessed Dec 18, 2012).

The Center for Biblical Counseling and Discipleship, http://www.center4biblicalcounseling.org/categories/PTSI/PT SI.html (accessed July 16, 2011).

Clark, Allen. "Treating PTSD". http://www.combatfaith.com/TreatingPTSD.html   (accessed June 20,2011).

Conrad, Bill. "Helping Out the Troops: Church's Boxes Include Items Such as Chips, Lip Balm." *Star Local News* (July 6, 2012) http://www.scntx.com/articles/ 2012/07/06/news_update/7016.txt (accessed Oct 26, 2012).

"Debunking Some Common Myths About Chaplaincy," (Aug 10,2010), http://sbcchaplain.wordpress.com/category/uncategorized, (accessed April 6, 2011).

Department of Defense Instruction 1304.28. *Guidance for the Appointment of Chaplains for the Military   Departments.* (June 11, 2004) http://www.dtic.mil/whs/directives/corres/pdf/130428p.pdf (accessed Nov 26,   2012).

Dickey, Christopher and Jessica Ramirez. "Love and War." *Newsweek* (Oct 13, 2007). http://www.thedailybeast.com/newsweek/2007/10/13/love-and-war.html (accessed Aug 23,2011)

Emert, Rick. "Lodge Offers Traditional Ceremonies" (Aug. 5, 2010) http://www.army.mil/article/43370/lodge-offers-traditional-ceremonies   (accessed Aug 2, 2011).

Evangelical Lutheran Church of America. "Blessing for Those Leaving for Military Service." http://archive.elca.org/worship/peace/ elca_blessing.html (accessed June 3, 2012).

Gilbert, Kathy L. "Chaplains: Church must support returning soldiers" *United Methodist News Service* (Feb. 20, 2007) http://www.umc.org/site/apps/nl/content3.asp?c=lwL4KnN1 LtH&b=2429867&ct=3574065 (accessed Dec. 13, 2012).

Gingerich, Melvin, and Paul Peachey. "Historic Peace Churches." *Global Anabaptist Mennonite Encyclopedia* Online. (1989). http:// www.gameo.org/encyclopedia/contents/H59ME.html (accessed October 26, 2012).

"The Good War and Those Who Refused to fight it: Non-combatant Medics," http://www.pbs.org/itvs/thegoodwar/field.html (accessed Oct 29,2012).

Granjo, Paulo. "The Homecomer: Postwar Cleansing Rituals in Mozambique." in *Armed Forces & Society* 33, no. 3 (April 2007): 382-395.

He Ska Akicita Inipi History. http:/ /www.cdprogramsites.org/synapse/ news fullstory_public.cfm?articleid=30835&website=cdprogramsites.o rg/kanasita (accessed July 30, 2011).

Huyser-Honig, Joan. "Becoming a Veteran-friendly Church: Pacifists Can Do This Too."(Oct 5, 2008) http://worship.calvin.edu/resources/resource-library/becoming-a-veteran-friendly-church-pacifists- can-do-this-too (accessed June 9, 2012).

Johansmeyer, Tom. "Operation Desert Porn" in Boston Magazine (July 2008) http://www.bostonmagazine.com/articles/operation_desert_po rn/page2 (accessed Aug 23, 2011).

Kaiser, Dakota J. "Combat Related Post Traumatic Stress Disorder in Veterans of Operation Enduring Freedom and Operation Iraqi Freedom: A Review of the Literature" (June 24, 2012) *Graduate Journal of Counseling Psychology,* Vol 3, no. 1, http://epublications.marquette.edu/gjcp/vol3/iss1/5 (accessed on Dec 18, 2012)

North American Missions Board of the Southern Baptist Convention. "A Biblical Response To Post-Traumatic Stress Disorder (PTSI)." (2009). http://www.namb.net/chaplaincyresources (accessed April 5, 2011).

Officers' Christian Fellowship. "Purpose Statement and Vision Statement of Officers' Christian Fellowship," http://www.ocfusa.org/abo purpose ut/, (accessed June 3, 2012).

Operation Barnabas. From the link "Service Of Welcome For A Returning Veteran." http://barnabas.lcmsworldmission.org/?page_id=624, (accessed Dec. 13, 2012).

Outback Steakhouse. "Feed the Troops," http://www.outback.com/companyinfo/feedingfreedom.aspx (accessed Oct 27, 2012).

Page, Bob. Transcript excerpt from VA course PTSD 101 entitled "Iraq Never Leaves Us." http://www.ptsd.va.gov/professional/ptsd101/ptsd101-pdf/Page_Transcript4-03-07.pdf (accessed Dec 17,2010).

Presbyterian Church, U.S.A. "Ceremony of Restoration." http://www.pcusa.org/resource/ceremony-restoration (accessed Dec. 17, 2012).

Presbyterian Church U.S.A. website, "Worship Rituals and Practices to Support Veterans" http://www.pcusa.org/media/uploads/phewa/pdfs/worship-rituals.pdf (accessed Dec. 17, 2012).

"RDK Shipments Pass 2.4 Million Mark!" (Mar 1, 2012) http://www.militaryministry.org/2012/03/01/rdk-shipments/ (accessed Oct 29,2012).

Rogers Petroleum. "Feed the Troops," http://www.rogerspetroleum.com/index2.php?option=com_content&do_pdf=1&id=8 (accessed Oct 26, 2012).

Rundgren, Karl. "Lee Greenwood Performs In Midland On Anniversary Of September 11th Attack", *Permianbasin360* (September 11, 2012) http://permianbasin360.com/fulltext?nxd_id=215102 (accessed Oct 25,2012).

Slack, Charles. "PTSD Timeline: Centuries of Trauma," *Protomag* (Summer 2010). http://protomag.com/assets/ptsd-timeline-centuries-of-traum (accessed Nov. 18, 2010).

"Spirituality" e-pamphlet for returning veterans. http://www.afterdeployment.org/media/elibrary/spirituality/index.html (accessed Dec 17, 2010).

Spotswood, Stephen. "Advocates Say 40 Percent of Vets Seek Counseling from Clergy and VA Partnership Could Help." *U.S. Medicine.* http:// www.usmedicine.com/articles/advocates-say-40-percent-of-vets-seek- counseling-from-clergy-and-va-partnership-could-help-.html (accessed November 17, 2012).

Tucker, Phebe and Elizabeth A. Foote, "Trauma and the Mind-Body Connection." June 1, 2007). *Psychiatric Times.* http://www.psychiatrictimes.com/mdd/content/article/10168/53811?pageNumber=2 (accessed Nov 26, 2012).

"Welcome Them Home- Help Them Heal Continues to Roll."
http://www.elimchurchblackhoof.org/news_detail.php?recordI
D=413 (accessed May 30, 2011).

Wunderink, Susan. "Not Just Chaplains." *Christianity Today* (Aug. 21,
2007).
http://www.christianitytoday.com/ct/2007/augustweb
only/134-22.0.html (accessed Mar 3, 2011).

ENDNOTES

[1] Bob Page, transcript excerpt from VA course PTSD 101 entitled "Iraq Never Leaves Us," http://www.ptsd.va.gov/professional/ptsd101/ptsd101-pdf/Page_Transcript4-03-07.pdf (accessed Dec 17,2010).

[2] "Spirituality" pamphlet for returning veterans, http://www.afterdeployment.org/media/elibrary/spirituality/index.html (accessed Dec 17, 2010).

[3] Department of Defense Instruction 1304.28, *Guidance for the Appointment of Chaplains for the Military Departments* (June 11, 2004), http://www.dtic.mil/whs/directives/corres/pdf/130428p.pdf (accessed Nov. 26, 2012).

[4] American Psychiatric Association, *Diagnostic and Statistical Manual of Mental Disorders, 4th ed., text rev.*(Washington, D.C. : American Psychiatric Association, 2000) 463.

[5] Terri Tanielian and Lisa H. Jaycox, eds. *The Invisible Wounds of War: Psychological and Cognitive Injuries, Their Consequences, and Services to Assist Recovery* (Santa Monica, CA: Rand Corporation, 2008), iii.

[6] Ibid., xxi.

[7] Ibid., 3.

[8] *DSM-IV-TR*, 463.

[9] William P. Nash, "The Stressors of War," in *Combat Stress Injury: Theory, Research, and Management*, edited by Charles R. Figley and William P. Nash (New York: Routledge, 2007), 27.

[10] *The Iraq War Clinician Guide*, 2nd ed., (National Center for PTSD, June 2004) 11.

[11] Jonathan Shay's *Achilles in Vietnam* and *Odysseus in America* trace the progression of PTSI through Homer's *The Iliad* and *The Odyssey*.

[12] Nu 31:19.

[13] Alan Fontana and Robert Rosenheck, "Trauma, Change in Strength of Religious Faith, and Mental Health Service Use Among Veterans Treated for PTSI," *The Journal of Nervous and Mental Disease* 192, no. 9 (September 2004): 579.

[14] Edward Tick, *War and the Soul: Healing Our Nation's Veterans From Post-Traumatic Stress Disorder* (Wheaton, Illinois: Quest Books, 2005), 209.

[15] Bosworth, David. "You have Shed Much Blood, and Waged Great Wars': Killing, Bloodguilt, and Combat Stress," *Journal of Religion, Disability & Health* 12 (3) (2008): 246.

[16] Ibid.

[17] Jonathan Shay, *Odysseus in America*, 245.

[18] Bosworth, David. "You have Shed Much Blood, and Waged Great Wars," 246.

[19] Joseph I. Blau, "The Red Heifer: A Biblical Purification Rite in Rabbinic Literature," *Numen 14,* no. 1 (1967): 72.

[20] Chad Brand, Charles Draper, and Archie England, eds *Holman's Illustrated Bible Dictionary,* s.v. "clean, cleanness," 361.

[21] Gal 3:10-13.

[22] Jonathan Shay, *Achilles in Vietnam*, 70.

[23] Patricia Kime, "Leadership's Progress on Suicide Appears to Lag," *Navy Times*, August 27, 2012.

[24] Jonathan Shay, *Odysseus in America*, 290.

[25] Jonathan Shay, *Odysseus in America*, 54; Patricia Kime, "Leadership's Progress on Suicide Appears to Lag," *Navy Times* (Aug 27, 2012) 12.

[26] Jonathan Shay, *Odysseus in America*, 245.

[27] David Bosworth, "You have Shed Much Blood, and Waged Great Wars," 247.

[28] John Sippola et al., *Welcome Them Home, Help Them Heal,* 45.

[29] Brown-Driver-Briggs, *Hebrew Definitions*, s.v. צלמות.

[30] Jacob Milgrom, "Encroaching on the Sacred: Purity and Polity in Numbers 1-10," *Interpretations* 51.3 (July 1997): 244.

[31] *Merriam-Webster's Collegiate Dictionary,* s.v. "contaminate."

[32] Aaron Beck et al, *Cognitive Therapy of Depression* (New York: The Guilford Press, 1979), 21.

[33] Brett T. Litz et al., "Moral Injury and Moral Repair: A Preliminary Model and Intervention Strategy," in *Clinical Psychology Review* 29 (2009): 697.

[34] *DSM-IV-TR*, 463

[35] Dakota J. Kaiser, "Combat Related Post-Traumatic Stress Disorder in Veterans of Operation Enduring Freedom and Operation Iraqi Freedom: A Review of the Literature" (June 24, 2012) *Graduate Journal of Counseling Psychology,* Vol 3, no. 1 http://epublications.marquette.edu/gjcp/vol3/iss1/5 (accessed on Dec 18, 2012)

[36] Gary S. Selby, "The Meaning and Function of συνείδησις in Hebrews 9 and 10," in *Restoration Quarterly* 28 no. 3 (1985-1986): 147.

[37] Harold S. Songer, "A Superior Priesthood: Hebrews 4:14-7:28" in *Review & Expositor* 82, no. 3 (Sum 1985): 351.

[38] Bernard J. Verkamp, *The Moral Treatment of Returning Warriors in Early Medieval and Modern Times* (Scranton: University of Scranton Press, 2006), 15.

[39] John Proctor, "Proselytes and Pressure Cookers: The Meaning and Application of Acts 15:20," *International Review of Mission* (Oct. 1, 1996): 472.

[40] Mark Allman, *Who Would Jesus Kill: War, Peace, and the Christian Tradition* (Winona, MN: Anselm Academic, 2008), 77.

[41] John T. McNeill and Helena M. Gamer. *Medieval Handbooks of Penance* (New York: Columbia University Press, 1990), 5.

[42] Tertullian, "On the Crown," Chap 11 quoted in Mark Allman, *Who Would Jesus Kill*, 80.

[43] Roland H. Bainton. *Christian Attitudes Toward War and Peace* (Nashville: Abbingdon Press, 1960), 85.

[44] Ibid., 86.

[45] Mark Allman, *Who Would Jesus Kill,* 83.

[46] Ibid.

[47] Roland H. Bainton, *Christian Attitudes Toward War and Peace,* 99.

[48] Augustine, *City of God,* Book 19, Chap 7, quoted in Mark Allman, *Who Would Jesus Kill,* 171.

[49] Darrell Cole, *Just War, Penance and the Church* Pro Ecclesia 11 no. 3 (Summer 2002): 316.

[50] Roland H. Bainton, *Christian Attitudes Toward War and Peace,* 97.

[51] Ibid., 92.

[52] Mark Allman, *Who Would Jesus Kill*, 167-168.

[53] Louis V. Iasiello, *Jus in Bellum: Key Issues for a Contemporary Assessment of Just Behavior in War*, (PhD diss., Salve Regina University, 2003), 10.

[54] Darrell Cole*, Just War, Penance and the Church*, 327.

[55] Bernard J. Verkamp, *The Moral Treatment of Returning Warriors in Early Medieval and Modern Times*, 23.

[56] Ibid., 10.

[57] Bernard J. Vernkamp, "Moral Treatment of Returning Warriors in the Early Middle Ages," *Journal of Religious Ethics* 16 no. 2 (Fall 1988): 229 and Darrell

Cole, *Just War, Penance and the Church*, 319.

[58] Darrell Cole, *Just War, Penance and the Church*, 323.

[59] Quoted in Roland H. Bainton's, *Christian Attitudes Toward War and Peace*, 78.

[60] Mark Allman, *Who Would Jesus Kill*, 171.

[61] Bernard J. Verkamp, *The Moral Treatment of Returning Warriors in Early Medieval and Modern Times*, 2.

[62] John T. McNeill and Helena M. Gamer, *Medieval Handbooks of Penance* (New York: Columbia University Press, 1938), 187, 225, 317.

[63] Ibid., 15.

[64] Zanchettin, Leo, ed., "A Sign that Heals," *The Word Among Us* 31, no. 6 (June 2012): 5.

[65] Darrell Cole, "Just War, Penance and the Church," *Pro Ecclesia* 11, no. 3 (Summer 2002): 322.

[66] Thomas E. Madden, "Inventing the Crusades," *First Things* (June/July 2009): 43.

[67] Chris Adsit, Rahnella Adsit, and Marshele Carter Waddell, *When War Comes Home: Christ-Centered Healing for Wives of Combat Veterans* (Newport News, Virginia: Military Ministry Press, 2008), 10.

[68] Chris Adsit, *The Combat Trauma Healing Manual: Christ-centered Solutions for Combat Trauma.* (Newport News, VA: Military Ministry Press, 2008), 39.

[69] Ibid.

[70] Ibid., 53.

[71] Ibid., 58.

[72] Ibid., 53.

[73] Ibid., 83.

[74] John Sippola et al, *Welcome Them Home Help Them Heal: Pastoral Care and Ministry with Service Members Returning from War* (Duluth, Minnesota: Whole Person Associates, 2009), 22.

[75] Ibid., 42.

[76] Ibid., 46.

[77] Ibid.

[78] Ibid., 50.

[79] John Sippola et al, *Welcome Them Home Help Them Heal,* 71.

[80] Ibid., 81.

[81] Ibid., 80.

[82] Ibid., 80 and 82.

[83] Operation Barnabas, From the link "Service Of Welcome For A Returning Veteran," http://barnabas.lcmsworldmission.org/?page_id=624 (accessed Dec. 13, 2012).

[84] Christopher Dorn and John Zemmler, "The Invisible Wounds of War: Post-Traumatic Stress Disorder and Liturgy in Conversation" in *Call to Worship* 43, no.2 (2009—2010): 6.

[85] Laura Bender, "An Order for Welcoming Service Members Returning from War." (May 2007), http://www.gbhem.org/site/apps/nlnet/content2.aspx?c=lsKSL3POLvF&b=5079785&ct=4969667 (Accessed on May 18,2011).

[86] Kathy L. Gilbert, "Chaplains: Church Must Support Returning Soldiers," *United Methodist News Service* (Feb. 20, 2007) http://www.umc.org/site/apps/nl/content3.asp?c=lwL4KnN1LtH&b=2429867&ct=3574065 (accessed Oct 27, 2012).

[87] Edward Tick, *War and the Soul,* 1.

[88] *Merriam-Webster's Collegiate Dictionary*, s.v. "contaminate."

[89] Christopher Dorn and John Zemmler, "The Invisible Wounds of War: Post Traumatic Stress Disorder and Liturgy in Conversation," *Call to Worship* 43.2 (2010): 2.

[90] *Merriam-Webster's Collegiate Dictionary*, s.v. "post" and "traumatic."

[91] Ibid., s.v. "stress" and "injury."

[92] William Nash, "Combat/Operational Stress Adaptations and Injuries," in *Combat Stress Injury: Theory, Research and Management,* edited by Charles R. Figley and William P. Nash (New York: Routledge, 2007), 36.

[93] Ibid., 53.

[94] Phebe Tucker and Elizabeth A. Foote, "Trauma and the Mind-Body Connection," (June 1, 2007) *Psychiatric Times* 24.7 http://www.psychiatrictimes.com/mdd/content/article/10168/53811?pageNumber=2 (accessed Nov 26, 2012).

[95] Joseph A. Boscarino, "The Mortality Impact of Combat Stress 30 Years after Exposure: Implications for Prevention, Treatment and Research" in *Combat Stress Injury: Theory, Research, and Management,* edited by Charles R. Figley and William P. Nash (New York: Routledge, 2007), 98.

[96] Eva Irle et al., "Reduced Amygdalar and Hippocampal Size in Adults with Generalized Social Phobia," *Journal of Psychiatry Neuroscience*, 35 (2) (2010): 126 .

[97] J. Douglas Bremmer, "Brain Imaging in Anxiety Disorders," in *Expert Review Neurotherapeutics* 4(2) (2004): 91.

[98] William P. Nash and Dewleen G. Baker, "Competing and Complementary Models of Combat Stress Injury," in *Combat Stress Injury: Theory, Research, and Management, edited by Charles R. Figley and William P. Nash (New York: Routledge, 2007),* 81.

[99] Ibid.

[100] J. Douglas Bremmer, "Brain Imaging in Anxiety Disorders," 91.

[101] Ibid., 92.

[102] William P. Nash and Dewleen G. Baker, "Competing and Complementary Models of Combat Stress Injury," in *Combat Stress Injury: Theory, Research, and Management,* 83.

[103] Jonathan Shay, *Achilles in Vietnam,* 170.

[104] William P. Nash and Dewleen G. Baker, "Competing and Complementary Models of Combat Stress Injury," in *Combat Stress Injury: Theory, Research, and Management,* 83.

[105] J. Douglas Bremmer, "Brain Imaging in Anxiety Disorders," 92.

[106] Ibid., 93.

[107] Ruth A. Lanius et al, "Does Neuroimaging Research Examining the Pathophysiology of Posttraumatic Stress Disorder Require Medication-free Patients?" in *Journal of Psychiatry and Neuroscience* 35.2 (March 2010): 80.

[108] William P. Nash and Dewleen G. Baker, "Competing and Complementary Models of Combat Stress Injury," 88.

[109] Eva Irle et al., "Reduced Amygdalar and Hippocampal Size in Adults with Generalized Social Phobia," *Journal of Psychiatry Neuroscience* 35 (2) (2010): 126.

[110] Matthew Alpers, *The God Part of the Brain: A Scientific Interpretation of Human Spirituality and God* (Naperville, Illinois: Sourcebooks Inc., 2006), 17.

[111] 1Co 15:44.

[112] *Brown-Driver-Brigg's Hebrew Dictionary*, s.v. נֶפֶשׁ.

[113] Ellis R. Brotzman, "Man and the Meaning of נֶפֶשׁ," *Bibliotheca sacra* 145, no. 580 (Oct-Dec 1988): 403.

[114] Christopher Dorn and John D. Zemler, "The Invisible Wounds of War," 2.

[115] *DSM-IV-TR*, 464.

[116] Jonathan Shay, *Achilles in Vietnam,* 23.

[117] Chris Adsit, *The Combat Trauma Healing Manual,* 11.

[118] *Spirituality,*
http://www.afterdeployment.org/media/elibrary/spirituality/index.html
(accessed Feb 16,2011).

[119] Edward Tick, *War and the Soul,* 209.

[120] Julia M. Whealin, "Warzone-related Stress Reactions: What Veterans Need to Know- A National Center for PTSI Fact Sheet," in *Iraq War Clinician Guide,* 29.

[121] *Merriam-Webster's Collegiate Dictionary*, s.v. "guilt."

[122] Jonathan Shay, *Achilles in Vietnam,* 5.

[123] Brett T. Litz et al., "Moral Injury and Moral Repair," 697.

[124] William P. Nash, "The Stressors of War" in *Combat Stress Injury: Theory, Research, and Management,* 26.

[125] Julia M. Whealin, "Warzone-related Stress Reactions: What Veterans Need to Know- A National Center for PTSI Fact Sheet," in *Iraq War Clinician Guide*, 191.

[126] Jonathan Shay, *Achilles in Vietnam*, 169.

[127] See Terri Tanielian and Lisa H. Jaycox. eds, *The Invisible Wounds of War: Psychological and Cognitive Injuries, Their Consequences, and Services to Assist Recover (*Santa Monica, CA: Rand Corporation, 2008), 12.

[128] American Psychiatric Association. "Practice Guideline for the Treatment of Patients with Major Depressive Disorder (revision)," *American Journal of Psychiatry* 157, no. 4 suppl., (April 2000): 4.

[129] Benjamin Wolman and George Stricker, eds, *"Depressive Disorders: Facts Theories, and Treatment Methods* (New York: John Wiley and Sons, 1990), 14.

[130] Aaron Beck et al, *Cognitive Therapy of Depression* (New York: The Guilford Press, 1979), 10.

[131] Ashley Hart, *An Operators Manual for Combat PTSI: Essays for Coping* (Lincoln, NE: iUniverse.Com, 2000), 53.

[132] Jonathan Shay, *Achilles in Vietnam,* 170.

[133] Aaron Beck et al, *Cognitive Therapy of Depression,* 12.

[134] *Merriam-Webster's Collegiate Dictionary,* s.v. "contaminate."

[135] Jonathan Shay, *Achilles in Vietnam*, 66.

[136] William P. Nash, *Combat Stress Injury*, 27.

[137] *DSM-IV-TR*, 463.

[138] Alan Fontana and Robert Rosenheck, "Trauma, Change in Strength of Religious Faith, and Mental Health Service Use Among Veterans Treated for PTSD," 579.

[139] *Strong's Concordance*, s.v. משכיל.

[140] Ibid., s.v. צלמות.

[141] Walter L. Michel, "SLMWT, 'Deep Darkness' or 'Shadow of Death'?" *Biblical Research,* 29 (1984): 12.

[142] William P. Nash, "Combat/Operational Stress Adaptations and Injuries," in *Combat Stress Injury*, 38.

[143] Charles Slack, "PTSD Timeline: Centuries of Trauma," *Protomag (Summer 2010),* http://protomag.com/assets/ptsd-timeline-centuries-of-trauma (accessed Nov. 18, 2010).

[144] Ibid.

[145] Charles R.Figley and William P. Nash, eds., *Combat Stress Injury,* 163.

[146] William P. Nash, "Combat/Operational Stress Adaptations and Injuries," in *Combat Stress Injury,* 33.

[147] Jonathan Shay, *Odysseus in America* and *Achilles, in Vietnam.*

[148] Robert J. Lifton, "Understanding the Traumatized Self: Imagery, Symbolization, and Transformation," in *Human Adaptation to Extreme Stress: From Holocaust to Vietnam,* eds. John P. Wilson, Zev Harel and Boaz Kahana (New York: Plenum Press, 1988): 18.

[149] Ibid.

[150] Jonathan Shay, *Achilles in Vietnam,* xx.

[151] Ibid., 5.

[152] Ibid.

[153] Ibid., 6.

[154] Brett T. Litz et al, "Moral Injury and Moral Repair," 697.

[155] Jonathan Shay, *Achilles in Vietnam,* 6.

[156] Ibid., 23.

[157] Ibid., 28.

[158] Ibid., 24.

[159] Ibid., 51.

[160] Ibid., 52.

[161] Ibid., 53.

[162] *Strong's Concordance,* s.v. יָשֻׁן.

[163] Jonathan Shay, *Achilles in Vietnam,* 69.

[164] William P. Nash, "The Stressors of War" in *Combat Stress Injury,* 26.

[165] Jonathan Shay, *Achilles in Vietnam,* 70.

[166] Ibid., 72.

[167] Ibid., 73.

[168] *Strong's Concordance*, s.v. כלמה .

[169] Ibid., s.v. תנין .

[170] Robert J. Lifton, "Understanding the Traumatized Self," 18.

[171] Jonathan Shay, *Achilles in Vietnam,* 88.

[172] Ibid., 98.

[173] Teresa Calpino, "The Gerasene Demoniac (Mark 5:1-20): the Pre-Markan Function of the Pericope," *Biblical Research* 53 (2008): 15.

[174] J Duncan M. Derrett, "Contributions To The Study Of The Gerasene Demoniac," *Journal for the Study of the New Testament* no. 3 (April 1979): 5.

[175] Teresa Calpino, "The Gerasene Demoniac (Mark 5:1-20)," 20.

[176] *Strong's Concordance* defines אלף as "a thousand". רבבה is defined as "a *myriad*, that is, indefinite *large number:* - ten . . . twenty thousand."

[177] Albert Barnes, *Notes on the New Testament,* Edited by Robert Frew. (Grand Rapids, MI: Baker Book House, 1949), s.v. Mt 4:24, Mt 8:28 and Mk 5:4.

[178] Ken Chamberlain, "The Gadarene Demoniac Finds Wholeness," *Journal of Pastoral Care & Counseling* 61 no 1-2 (Spring-Summer 2007): 134.

[179] H.W. Montefiore, *The Epistle to the Hebrews* (London: A & C Black, 1987), 66.

[180] *Strong's Concordance,* s.v. ἀλλάσσω.

[181] Heb 6:1-2; Heb 9:13-14.

[182] See ἀπαλλάσσω in Heb 2:15; μετανοιας in Heb 6:2; συνειδησιν in Heb 9:14.

[183] Charles R. Marmar and Mardi J. Horowitz, "Diagnosis and Phase-Oriented Treatment of Post-Traumatic Stress Disorder," in *Human Adaptation to Extreme Stress,* 90.

[184] Jonathan Shay, *Achilles in Vietnam,* xxii.

[185] Charles R. Marmar and Mardi J. Horowitz, "Diagnosis and Phase-Oriented Treatment of Post-Traumatic Stress Disorder," 91.

[186] Jonathan Shay, *Achilles in Vietnam,* 77.

[187] National Center for PTSD Fact Sheet, "Common Reactions to PTSD."

[188] Teresa Calpino, "The Gerasene Demoniac (Mk 5:1-20)," 17.

[189] National Center for PTSD Fact Sheet, "Common Reactions to PTSD."

[190] Jonathan Shay, *Achilles in Vietnam,* 70.

[191] North American Missions Board of the Southern Baptist Convention, "A Biblical Response To Post-Traumatic Stress Disorder (PTSI)," (2009), http://www.namb.net/chaplaincyresources (accessed April 5, 2011): 2.

[192] The Center for Biblical Counseling and Discipleship, http://www.center4biblicalcounseling.org/categories/PTSI/PTSI.html (accessed July 16, 2011).

[193] Steven Lugar, "Flood, Salt, and Sacrifice: Post Traumatic Stress Disorders in Genesis," *Jewish Bible Quarterly* 38.2 (Apr. 2010): 124.

[194] Southern Baptist Convention, "A Biblical Response To Post-Traumatic Stress Disorder (PTSI)." 20, http://www.namb.net/chaplaincyresources/ (accessed April 5, 2011).

[195] *DSM-IV-TR,* 467-468.

[196] Ibid., 463.

[197] Jon Courson, *Jon Courson's Application Commentary: Old Testament, vol. 1, Genesis-Job* (Nashville: Nelson, 2005), 81.

[198] W. Gunther Plaut, *The Torah: A Modern Commentary-Genesis* (New York: The Union of American Hebrew Congregations, 1972), 179.

[199] Ibid. 369.

[200] William P. Nash, "Combat/Operational Stress Adaptations and Injuries," 49.

[201] *DSM-III,* s.v. "Post-Traumatic Stress Disorder," quoted in "The Psychological Effects of Being a Prisoner of War" by American Psychiatric Association, "The Psychological Effects of Being a Prisoner of War" by American Psychiatric Association, *Human Adaptation to Extreme Stress,* 166., 166.

[202] Stephane Grenier et al., " The Operational Stress Injury Social Support Program: A Peer Support Program in Collaboration between the Canadian Forces and Veterans Affairs Canada," in *Combat Stress Injury,* eds. Charles R. Figley and William P. Nash, (New York: Routledge, 2007), 286.

[203] Ashley B. Hart II. *An Operators Manual for Combat PTSI: Essays for Coping* (New York: iUniverse.com, 2000), 50.

[204] Jephthah is threatened with this technique (Jdg 12:1) and it is used by Abimelech in Jdg 9:49.

[205] Robert G. Boling, *The Anchor Bible: Judge* (New York: Doubleday, 1975), 250.

[206] Jon Courson, *Jon Courson's Application Commentary: Old Testament,* vol. 1, 1016.

[207] Ashley B. Hart II. *An Operators Manual for Combat PTSD*, 11.

[208] American Psychiatric Association, *Diagnostic and Statistical Manual of Mental Disorders-III,* 248.

[209] Bret A. Moore and Greg M. Reger, "Historical and Contemporary Perspectives of Combat Stress and Army Combat Stress Control Team," in *Combat Stress Injury,* eds. Charles R. Figley and William P. Nash, 163.

[210] Joseph I. Blau, "The Red Heifer: A Biblical Purification Rite in Rabbinic Literature," *Numen* 14, no 1 (Mar 1967): 72.

[211] *Strong's Concordance,* s.v. מגן.

[212] T.K. Thomas, "Melchizedek, King and Priest: An Ecumenical Paradigm?" *The Ecumenical Review* 52 no. 3 (July 2000): 405-406.

[213] Brett T. Litz et al., "Moral Injury and Moral Repair: A Preliminary Model and Intervention Strategy," *Clinical Psychology Review* 29 (2009): 695-706.

[214] KJV translation of Ge 14:17.

[215] *Strong's Concordance,* s.v. מגן

[216] Mt 26:47-56; Mk 14:43-52; Lk 22:47-54; Jn 18:1-12.

[217] *Strong's Concordance,* s.v. מגן "figuratively to *rescue,* to *hand* safely *over* (that is, *surrender*): - deliver."

[218] Laura Bender, "An Order for Blessing Service Members Deploying to War," on the United Methodist Church Chaplain's webpage, http://www.gbhem.org/site/apps/nlnet/content2.aspx?c=lsKSL3POLvF&b=5079785&ct=4969669 (accessed June 3, 2012).

[219] Presbyterian Church, U.S.A., "Ceremony of Restoration," http://www.pcusa.org/resource/ceremony-restoration (June 3, 2012).

[220] Evangelical Lutheran Church of America, "Blessing for Those Leaving for Military Service," http://archive.elca.org/worship/peace/elca_blessing.html (accessed June 3, 2012).

[221] "An Order for Welcoming Service Members Returning from War," http://www.gbhem.org/site/apps/nlnet/content2.aspx?c=lsKSL3POLvF&b=5079785&ct=4969667 (Accessed May 18, 2011).

[222] Christopher Dorn and John Zemmler, "The Invisible Wounds of War: Post-Traumatic Stress Disorder and Liturgy in Conversation," *Call to Worship* 43.2 (2009-2010) 1-8.

[223] Presbyterian Church U.S.A. website, "Worship Rituals and Practices to support Veterans," http://www.pcusa.org/media/uploads/phewa/pdfs/worship-rituals.pdf (accessed June 6, 2012).

[224] Joan Huyser-Honig, "Becoming a Veteran-friendly Church: Pacifists Can Do This Too," http://worship.calvin.edu/resources/resource-library/becoming-a-veteran-friendly-church-pacifists-can-do-this-too (accessed June 9, 2012).

[225] Bobby Ross Jr., "Scripture Tags Offer Hope, Comfort to Soldiers in Iraq." *The Houston Chronicle* (Nov. 16, 2003).

[226] "Shields of Strength" offered on Amazon's Website. http://www.amazon.com/Shields-Strength-Battle-Shield-Dog/dp/B007VOOHZ2 (accessed June 4, 2012).

[227] Presbyterian Church U.S.A. website "Worship Rituals and Practices to support Veterans."

[228] Peggy Joyce Ruth and Angelia Ruth Schum, *Psalm 91: God's Shield of Protection* (Sisters, Oregon: The 1687 Foundation, 2009), 10.

[229] Statement made on a commercial website for Roman Catholic religious items, http://www.catholiccompany.com/blog/st-michael-medal-powerful-gift-military-personnel (accessed June 4, 2012).

[230] "Ten Tough Facts about Combat: And What Leaders Can Do to Mitigate Risk and Build Resilience," by Walter Reed Army Institute of Research of the U.S. Army Medical Research and Material Command (N.p., March 27, 2006).

[231] Ibid.

[232] *Merriam-Webster's Collegiate Dictionary,* s.v. "morale."

[233] Patrick S. Gilmore, "When Johnny Comes Marching Home," 1863 and Daniel Decatur Emmett, "Dixie," 1859.

[234] Julia Ward Howe, "Battle Hymn of the Republic," 1861.

[235] C. Michael Hawn, "Battle-Hymn Inspired by Visit to Troops in Civil War," *The United Methodist Reporter* (July 4, 2012) http://www.unitedmethodistreporter.com/2012/07/battle-hymn-inspired-by-visit-to-troops-in-civil-war/ (accessed Oct 27, 2012).

[236] Frank Loesser, "Praise the Lord and Pass the Ammunition," Famous Music Corp., 1942.

[237] Ibid.

[238] Darryl Worley, "Have You Forgotten," (Nashville: DreamWorks, 2003).

[239] Toby Keith, "Angry American: Courtesy of the Red, White and Blue" on "Unleashed" (Nashville: DreamWorks Records, 2002).

[240] Karl Rundgren, "Lee Greenwood Performs In Midland On Anniversary Of September 11th Attack," *Permianbasin360* (September 11, 2012) http://permianbasin360.com/fulltext?nxd_id=215102 (accessed Oct 25,2012).

[241] *Strong's Concordance,* s.v שאל

[242] Barbara E. Organ, "Pursuing Phinehas: A Synchronic Reading," *The Catholic Biblical Quarterly* 63 (2001): 213.

[243] Jacob Milgrom, *The JPS Torah Commentary: Numbers* (Philadelphia: The Jewish Publication Society, 1990), 257.

[244] James Turner Johnson, "The Quest for Peace: Three Moral Traditions in Western Cultural History" quoted in *Who Would Jesus Kill* by Mark J. Allman, (Winona, Minnesota: Anselm Academic, 2008), 79.

[245] Paul Christopher, *The Ethics of War and Peace: An Introduction to Legal and Moral Issues* (Englewood Cliffs, New Jersey: Prentice Hall Inc, 1994), 7.

[246] *Catechism of the Catholic Church*: *Pocket Edition* (London: Geoffrey Chapman, 1995), paragraph 2309.

[247] CDR Neal Moquin, "Personal Combat Readiness: Moral, Mental, and Emotional Fitness," a presentation provided to 4th Marine Corps Air Wing. Undated (N.p).

[248] Brett T. Litz et al, "Moral Injury and Moral Repair," 695-706.

[249] "RDK Shipments Pass 2.4 Million Mark!" (Mar 1, 2012) http://www.militaryministry.org/2012/03/01/rdk-shipments/ (accessed Oct 29,2012).

[250] Adelle M. Banks, "Southern Baptists Convention fighting 'don't ask, don't tell' repeal," Washington Post (June 19, 2010) http://www.washingtonpost.com/wp-dyn/content/article/2010/06/18/AR2010061804890.html (accessed Mar 11, 2011).

[251] Ibid.

[252] "Debunking Some Common Myths About Chaplaincy," (Aug 10,2010) http://sbcchaplain.wordpress.com/category/uncategorized (accessed April 6, 2011).

[253] Officers' Christian Fellowship, "Purpose Statement and Vision Statement of Officers' Christian Fellowship," http://www.ocfusa.org/about/purpose (accessed June 3, 2012).

[254] Navigators. "About Us," http://www.navigators.org/us/ministries/military (June 3, 2012).

[255] Barbara E. Organ, "Pursuing Phinehas," 213.

[256] Stephen Mansfield, *The Faith of the American Soldier* (Lake Mary, Florida: Front Line, 2005), 62.

[257] Stephen Mansfield, *The Faith of the American Soldier*, 59.

[258] From *The Warrior's Journey Home* website, http://www.warriorsjourneyhome.org/What_We_Do.html> (accessed June 18, 2011).

[259] From *Soldier's Heart* homepage, http://www.soldiersheart.net/index.shtml (accessed June 18, 2011).

[260] *The Warrior's Journey Home* website.

[261] Rick Emert, "Lodge Offers Traditional Ceremonies," http://www.army.mil/article/43370/lodge-offers-traditional-ceremonies (accessed Aug 2, 2011).

[262] Bruce McNair, "Luther, Calvin and the Exegetical Tradition of Melchisedec," *Review and Expositor* 101 (Fall 2004): 751.

[263] Ibid.

[264] Outback Steakhouse, "Feed the Troops," http://www.outback.com/companyinfo/feedingfreedom.aspx (Oct 27, 2012) and Rogers Petroleum "Feed the Troops" http://www.rogerspetroleum.com/index2.php?option=com_content&do_pdf=1&id=8 (accessed Oct 26, 2012).

[265] From the homepage of The Fellowship Church, Grapevine, TX http://www.fellowshipchurch.com/military (accessed Oct 26, 2012).

[266] Bill Conrad, "Helping Out the Troops: Church's Boxes Include Items Such as Chips, Lip Balm," *Star Local News* (July 6, 2012) http://www.scntx.com/articles/2012/07/06/news_update/7016.txt (accessed Oct 26, 2012).

[267] Ibid.

[268] Public Law 106-65.

[269] Thomas E. Darling, "Office of the Chaplain: Duties and Responsibilities," *Veterans of Foreign Wars Department Convention,* Washington D.C (June 18-21, 2008), 12-13.

[270] Ibid., 11

[271] "Special Memorial Day Service at Big Prairie Church," *Carmi Times* (May 23, 2012) http://www.carmitimes.com/article/20120523/NEWS/305239977 (accessed Oct 29, 2012).

[272]

http://www.goldstarmoms.com/Events/WreathsAcrossAmerica/WAA2010/WreathsAcrossAmerica2010.htm (accessed Oct 26, 2012).

[273] *Strong's Concordance,* s.v. יצא.

[274] Melvin Gingerich and Paul Peachey, "Historic Peace Churches," *Global Anabaptist Mennonite Encyclopedia* Online. (1989) http://www.gameo.org/encyclopedia/contents/H59ME.html (accessed October 26, 2012).

[275] "The Good War and Those Who Refused to fight it: Non-combatant Medics," http://www.pbs.org/itvs/thegoodwar/field.html (accessed Oct 29,2012).

[276] Joan Huyser-Honig, "Becoming a Veteran-friendly Church: Pacifists Can Do This Too," http://worship.calvin.edu/resources/resource-library/becoming-a-veteran-friendly-church-pacifists-can-do-this-too (accessed June 9, 2012).

[277] Kathy L. Gilbert, "Chaplains: Church Must Support Returning Soldiers," *United Methodist News Service* (Feb. 20, 2007). http://www.umc.org/site/apps/nl/content3.asp?c=lwL4KnN1LtH&b=2429867&ct=3574065 (accessed Oct 27, 2012).

[278] The United Methodist Church, "Social Principles of the United Methodist Church," paragraph165, *The Discipline of the United Methodist Church* (Nashville: The United Methodist Publishing House, 2008 .

[279] *Catechism of the Catholic Church*, 615.

[280] Pontifical Council for Justice and Peace, *Compendium of the Social Doctrine of the Church,* (Washington, D.C. : USCCB Publishing, 2004), 217.

[281] Leo Zanchettin, ed., "A Sign that Heals," *The Word Among Us* 31, no. 6 (June 2012), 5.

[282] Laura Bender, "An Order for Welcoming Service Members Returning from War."

[283] Christopher Dorn and John Zemmler, "The Invisible Wounds of War: Post-Traumatic Stress Disorder and Liturgy in Conversation," *Call to Worship,* 6.

[284] The World Council of Churches (WCC) is the broadest and most inclusive among the many organized expressions of the modern ecumenical movement. The WCC brings together 349 churches, denominations and church fellowships

in more than 110 countries and territories throughout the world, representing over 560 million Christians.

[285] Quoted from World Council of Churches, http://www.oikoumene.org/en/who-are-we.html (accessed April 23, 2009).

[286] T.R. Hobbs, *A Time for War: A Study of Warfare in the Old Testament* (Wilmington, Delaware: Michael Glazier, 1989), 13.

[287] *Strong's Concordance*, s.v. רעה.

[288] Chris Adsit, *The Combat Trauma Healing Manual: Christ-centered Solutions for Combat Trauma* (Newport News, VA: Military Ministry Press, 2008), 39.

[289] John Sippola et al., *Welcome Them Home Help Them Heal: Pastoral Care and Ministry with Service Members Returning from War* (Duluth, Minnesota: Whole Person Associates, 2009), 43.

[290] Ibid., 45

[291] Ibid., 71

[292] Ibid., 80-81

[293] *Strong's Concordance*, s.v. אסף.

[294] Explanation of the contents in *Welcome Them Home, Help Them Heal* from http://welcomethemhomebook.com/?page_id=16 (accessed June 3, 2012).

[295] "Worship Rituals and Practices to support Veterans," http://www.pcusa.org/media/uploads/phewa/pdfs/worship-rituals.pdf.

[296] Ibid.

[297] John Sippola et al., *Welcome Them Home Help Them Heal.*

[298] "Welcome Them Home- Help Them Heal Continues to Roll," http://www.elimchurchblackhoof.org/news_detail.php?recordID=413 (May 30, 2011).

[299] John Sippola et al., *Welcome Them Home Help Them Heal,* 79.

[300] Susan Wunderink, "Not Just Chaplains," *Christianity Today* (Aug 21, 2007), http://www.christianitytoday.com/ct/2007/augustweb-only/134-22.0.html (accessed Mar 3, 2011).

[301] Chris Adsit, *The Combat Trauma Healing Manual.*

[302] Bill Bright, "The 4 Spiritual Laws," New Life Publications, Orlando Florida (1965), http://4laws.com/laws/english/flash/ (accessed June 9, 2012).

[303] Chris Adsit, *The Combat Trauma Healing Manual,* 33.

[304] Allen Clark, "Treating PTSD," http://www.combatfaith.com/TreatingPTSD.html, (accessed June 20,2011).

[305] *Strong's Concordance,* s.v. חטא.

[306] David P. Wright, "Purification from Corpse-Contamination in Numbers XXXI, 19-24," *Vetus Testamentum* 35, 2 (1985), 214.

[307] Joseph L. Blau, "The Red Heifer: A Biblical Purification Rite in Rabbinic Literature," Numen 14, no.1 (Mar 1967): 71.

[308] See Chapter Three, page 50 of this study.

[309] Jonathan Shay, *Achilles in Vietnam,* 70.

[310] *Strong's Concordance,* s.v. νεκρῶν and ἔργων.

[311] Gary S. Selby, "The Meaning and Function of Συνείδησις in Hebrews 9 and 10," 147.

[312] Until cleansed a person who was contaminated by exposure to death could not approach the Tabernacle (Num 19:14). In early Judaism the Tabernacle was the access point of Yahweh worship and was located in the center of the camp.

[313] Joseph H. Thayer, *Thayer's Greek-English Lexicon of the New Testament,* s.v. συνείδησις.

[314] *Strong's Concordance,* s.v. συνείδω.

[315] Gary S. Selby, "The Meaning and Function of Συνείδησις in Hebrews 9 and 10", 145.

[316] Heb 9:9; 9:14; 10:2; 10:22; 13:18.

[317] Gary S. Selby, "The Meaning and Function of Συνείδησις in Hebrews 9 and 10," 147.

[318] Alan Fontana and Robert Rosenheck, "Trauma, Change in Strength of Religious Faith, and Mental Health Service Use Among Veterans Treated for PTSD," 579.

[319] Gary S. Selby, "The Meaning and Function of Συνείδησις in Hebrews 9 and 10," 150.

[320] Jonathan Shay, *Odysseus in America,* 245.

[321] David Bosworth, "You have Shed Much Blood, and Waged Great Wars': Killing, Bloodguilt, and Combat Stress," *Journal of Religion, Disability & Health* 12 (3), (2008), 246.

[322] Ibid. 245.

[323] *DSM-IV-TR*, 468

[324] "Confronting Trauma Directly Most Effective for PTSD," *World Disease Weekly* (May 17, 2005) General OneFile. Web. (July 27, 2011): 1383.

[325] *Merriam-Webster's Collegiate Dictionary*, s.v. "liturgy."

[326] Herbert Anderson, "How Rituals Heal," *Word and World* 30, no. 1 (Winter 2010): 42.

[327] Ibid.

[328] Ibid.

[329] Paulo Granjo, "The Homecomer: Postwar Cleansing Rituals in Mozambique," in *Armed Forces & Society* 33 no. 3 (April 2007): 389.

[330] Ibid., 382-395.

[331] Ibid., 382.

[332] Ibid., 392.

[333] "He Ska Akicita Inipi History,"
http://www.cdprogramsites.org/synapse/news/fullstory_public.cfm?articleid=
30835&website=cdprogramsites.org/kanasita (accessed July 30, 2011).

[334] Paula Bidwell, "Native American Sweat Lodge 'Inipi' Ceremony," *Ezine Articles,* http://ezinearticles.com/?Native-American-Sweat-Lodge-Inipi-Ceremony&id=2089226 (accessed Aug 2, 2011).

[335] Ibid.

[336] "He Ska Akicita Inipi History."

[337] Rick Emert, "Lodge Offers Traditional Ceremonies," on the official U.S. Army homepage, http://www.army.mil/article/43370/lodge-offers-traditional-ceremonies/ (accessed Aug 2, 2011).

[338] Ibid.

[339] Elaine Ramshaw, *Ritual and Pastoral Care,* ed. Don S.Browning (Philadelphia: Fortress Press, 1987), 16.

[340] "Confession of Faith of the Evangelical United Brethren Church, Article IV," *The Discipline of the United Methodist Church* (Nashville: The United Methodist Publishing House, 2008): 67.

[341] Joseph I. Blau, "The Red Heifer: A Biblical Purification Rite in Rabbinic Literature," 72.

[342] Jacob Neusner, trans., *The Mishnah: The New Translation,* (New Haven, CT: Yale University Press, 1988) 1016.

[343] Ibid.

[344] Heb 5:6; 5:10; 6:20; 7:11; 7:15; 7:17 and 7:21.

[345] *Strong's Concordance,* s.v. "κοινωνία".

[346] David P. Wright, "Purification from Corpse-Contamination in Numbers XXXI 19-24," *Vetus Testamentum* 35, 2 (1985), 214.

[347] Herbert Anderson, "How Rituals Heal," *Word and World*, 47.

[348] Roy A. Rappaport, "Ritual Time and Eternity" in *Zygon* 27, no 1 (March 1992):10.

[349] *Merriam-Webster's Collegiate Dictionary*, s.v. "mission."

[350] Robin Green, *Only Connect,* 58.

[351] Edward Tick, *War and the Soul,* 62.

[352] Robin Green, *Only Connect,* 5.

[353] Jonathan Shay, *Achilles in Vietnam,* 68.

[354] Edward Tick, *War and the Soul,* 140.

[355] Chris Adsit, *The Combat Trauma Healing Manual,* 66.

[356] Jonathan Shay, *Achilles in Vietnam*, 59.

[357] Ibid., 73.

[358] Brett T. Litz et al., "Moral Injury and Moral Repair: A Preliminary Model and Intervention Strategy," *Clinical Psychology Review* 29 (2009): 695-706.

[359] From Navy Chaplain training booklet, "Combat Operation Stress First Aid" (2009) Appendix L (n.p.)

[360] Jonathan Shay, *Odysseus in America*, 240.

[361] Jonathan Shay, "Casualties." *Daedalus* 140.3 (2011): 183

[362] Joint Service Committee on Military Justice, *The Manual for Courts-Martial United States*, Article 94—Mutiny and Sedition. (2002 edition).

[363] T. Andrew Taylor and Michael E. Sherr, "When Veterans Come Home," *Family and Community Ministries,* 21 no. 3 (Winter 2008): 9.

[364] Cited by Shay in "Casualties." *Daedalus* 140.3 (2011) 185.

[365] Christopher Dickey and Jessica Ramirez, "Love and War," in *Newsweek,* (Oct 13, 2007) http://www.thedailybeast.com/newsweek/2007/10/13/love-and-war.html (Aug 23,2011).

[366] Ibid.

[367] Tom Johansmeyer, "Operation Desert Porn," in *Boston Magazine* (July 2008) http://www.bostonmagazine.com/articles/operation_desert_porn/page2 (Aug 23, 2011).

[368] John Proctor, "Proselytes and Pressure-Cookers: The Meaning and Application of Acts 15:20," *International Review of Mission 85*, no. 339 (Oct. 1, 1996): 471.

[369] *Strong's Concordance,* s.v. "πορνεύω."

[370] William M. Struthers, *Wired for Intimacy*, (Downers Grove, IL: Intervarsity Press, 2009), 42.

[371] Southern Baptist Convention, "A Biblical Response To Post-Traumatic Stress Disorder (PTSD)," 20, http://www.namb.net/chaplaincyresources/ (accessed April 5, 2011).

[372] Jonathan Shay, *Odysseus in America*,161.

[373] *Strong's Concordance*, s.v. דבר.

[374] Robyn Walser et al., *Acceptance and Commitment Therapy*, p.13.

[375] Ibid., 13.

[376] Rebecca Dana, "@$#&*% Ken Burns! PBS Scrubbing G.I. Mouths With Soap," *New York Observer* (Oct. 2, 2006):   .

[377] John Sippola et al., *Welcome Them Home Help Them Heal*, p. 50.

[378] Rupert Hamer, "Faith on the Iraq Frontline; REMEMBER OUR HEROES," *Sunday Mirror,* Nov. 11, 2007.

379 The verb Jesus uses for "deny" is nearly an antonym to "conscience," *Thayer's A Greek-English Lexicon of the New Testament,* - ἀπαρνέομαι – "deny . . . to lose sight of one's self." *Strong's Concordance*- συνείδησις : "a prolonged form of συνείδω . . . conscience . . . to see completely."

380 A. M. Stibbs, *The Meaning of the Word 'Blood' in Scripture* (3rd ed ; London: Tyndale, 1962), 30.

381 Stephen Spotswood, "Advocates say 40 percent of Vets Seek Counseling From Clergy and VA Partnership Could Help, " *U.S. Medicine,* http://www.usmedicine.com/articles/advocates-say-40-percent-of-vets-seek-counseling-from-clergy-and-va-partnership-could-help-.html (accessed November 17, 2012).

382 *DSM-IV-TR*, 467-468.

383 Terri Tanielian and Lisa H. Jaycox, eds. *The Invisible Wounds of War: Psychological and Cognitive Injuries, Their Consequences, and Services to Assist Recovery,* (Santa Monica, CA: Rand Corporation, 2008), 3.

384 Mat 8:8 CEV.

385 Num 31:4.

386 Num 31:49.

387 MIA = Missing in Action.

388 Joint Service Committee on Military Justice, *The Manual for Courts-Martial United States*, Article 94—Mutiny and Sedition. (2002 edition).

389 Num 31:14.

390 Jonathan Shay, *Achilles in Vietnam: Combat Trauma and the Undoing of Character.* (New York: Scribner, 1994), 6.

391 Num 31:15--16.

392 Num 31:25--27.

393 1 Sam 30:24.

[394] These are just two of many documents that set the parameters for the Law of Land Warfare used by the U.S. military.

[395] *Strong's Concordance*, s.v. דבר.

[396] Rebecca Dana, "@$#&*% Ken Burns! PBS Scrubbing G.I. Mouths With Soap," *New York Observer* (Oct. 2, 2006): 1.

[397] John Sippola et al., *Welcome Them Home Help Them Heal*, p. 50.

[398] Rupert Hamer, "Faith on the Iraq Frontline; REMEMBER OUR HEROES." *Sunday Mirror* (Nov. 11, 2007).

[399] Robyn Walser et al., *Acceptance and Commitment Therapy*, p.13.

[400] Ibid., p.13

[401] Num 19:14.

[402] Num 19:13.

[403] Num 31:19-20.

[404] Num 19:13.

[405] Heb 9:14.

[406] Psalm 51:6-10 ESV.

[407] Matt 8:2--3.